# THE SIGNS
# THE DA
# JUDGEMENT

بسم الله الرحمن الرحيم

In the name of Allah, All-Merciful and Compassionate

IBN KATHĪR

DAR AL TAQWA LTD.

Reprinted 1997

ISBN 1 870582 039



Translation: Mrs Huda Khattab

Editorial: Muhammad Isa Waley

Published by:
Dar Al Taqwa Ltd.
7A, Melcombe Street
Baker Street
London
NW1 6AE
email: dar.altaqwa@btinternet.com

Printed and Bound by- De-Luxe Printers,
London NW10 7NR.
website: http://www.de-luxe.com
email: naresh@aapi.co.uk

# Contents

# Introduction

Ibn Kathīr, a scholar of many Islamic sciences, is best known as a commentator of the Qur'ān (*mufassir*), historian and narrator of prophetic tradition.

He has three honorific titles: *al-Imām*, the leader, *al-Ḥāfiẓ*, the preserver of the prophetic tradition, and 'Imād al-Din, pillar of the religion.

The words *al-Qurayshī*, *al-Dimashqī* and *al-Shāfi'ī* are sometimes attached to his name. The first shows his Meccan roots, the second indicates the city (Damascus) in which he spent most of his life, and the last the school of law he followed.

His full name was Ismā'īl Abū'l-Faḍl 'Umar Ibn Kathīr.

He was born in al-Mujaddal, a village east of Busra in the province of Damascus (Syria), at the turn of the eighth century after the Prophet's migration (702 AH/ 1300 AD). There is disagreement about his exact year of birth:: all years between 698 and 702 AH (1296 – 1300 AD) have been suggested. He recorded memories of his father who is believed to have died in 703 AH. A few years after his father's death, at the age of about seven or eight, he moved to Damascus.

Damascus was at that time a stronghold of orthodox Islam. It was the home of many learned men and offered the opportunity to study the Islamic sciences to an advanced level. Ibn Kathīr took advantage of this and the environment brought out the best in his developing mind.

He first studied jurisprudence (*fiqh*) under Burhān al-Dīn al-Fazariyyah and Kamāl al-Dīn ibn Qāḍi. He then married into the family of Abū'l Ḥajjāj al-Māzī, from whom he studied *Ḥadīth* (Prophetic tradition). His most famous teacher was Taqī al-Dīn Ibn Taymiyyah, from whom he learned many *Aḥādīth* and who influenced many of his legal judgements. His teacher died when Ibn Kathīr was 28 years old. He therefore witnessed the last ten years of the great jurist's life, which were marked by intermittent persecution.

After Ibn Taymiyyah's death Ibn Kathīr's own reputation grew. He was soon to become one of the most respected scholars of the whole region. He was best known for his recall of *Aḥādīth* and his ability to explain them with all the relevant details that made the whole event clear to his students.

The title *'al-Ḥāfiẓ'* is only given to a scholar who has memorised the text and chain of narrators of the *Ḥadīth*, along with relevant information that gives full comprehension (*dirāyah*) of the *Ḥadīth*. Ibn Kathīr had done this at an early age. His student, al-Ḥāfiẓ Ibn Ḥijjī said 'He had memorised the most *Aḥādīth* of all the narrators of *Ḥadīth* I had ever met.'

This vast reservoir of tradition was the source for his many writings. They included books on jurisprudence, history and the science of *Ḥadīth* studies. His famous commentary on the Qur'ān, *Tafsīr al-Qur'ān al-'Aẓīm* is one of the most authoritative exegeses. In the preface he explains his method and sets out a system which was to be adhered to by all serious commentators. He protected the integrity of the science of exegesis.

He died on Thursday 26th of Sha'bān 774 AH (1373 AD) and was buried in the graveyard of Ṣūfiyyah with his teacher Ibn Taymiyyah.

This book is an extract from his book *al-Bidāyah wa'l-nihāyah*. *Al-Bidāyah* is a history book which has three main sections. It begins with the pre-Islamic period and explains how the climate of *Jāhiliyyah* (ignorance) came about. This section describes the revelation of the Qur'ān, the persecution of the Muslims and the setting up of the first Islamic community in Madīnah. The second section covers the period of the Rightly Guided Caliphs and the Muslim dynasties up to, and including, the time of the author. The final section describes the end of the world as narrated in *Ḥadīth* literature. Both his commentary and history book were useful contributions to the scholarly community of Damascus. However, the structure of these masterpieces makes them relevant to all Muslims, regardless of their time and situation.

'The Signs of The Day of Judgement' has been edited during translation to make it as relevant as possible to the modern English-speaking reader. The *Aḥādīth* have been limited to those dealing directly with The Day of Judgement and the signs, warnings and disasters which will occur shortly before it. The main purpose in translating this book is to show that events occurring every day are not happening by chance, but are part of the Creator's overall plan. These are events which will eventually lead to the Last Day when every human being will stand in judgement for their previous actions.

The book should instil the loving awe that will take us beyond that great event. It is this awareness that will, *inshā' Allāh* bring us into His Garden and save us from His Fire – the two ultimate consequences of judgement.

'The Signs of The Day of Judgement' will be beneficial to all who truly look forward to meeting their Lord. May Allah SWT shower His Mercy upon the author of this book.

Chapter 1

# *ĀYĀT* AND *AḤĀDĪTH* ABOUT THE HOUR

Allah SWT said:

> "They ask thee about the Hour, 'When will be its appointed time?' Wherein art thou (concerned) with the declaration thereof? With thy Lord is the Limit fixed therefor. Thou art but a Warner for such as fear it. The Day they will see it, (it will be) as if they had tarried but a single evening, or (at most till) the following morn!"
> (*al-Nāzi'āt* 79:42-46)
>
> "They ask thee about the (final) Hour – when will be its appointed time? Say: 'The knowledge thereof is with my Lord (alone): none but He can reveal as to when it will occur. Heavy were its burden through the heavens and the earth. Only, all of a sudden will it come to you.' They ask thee as if thou wert eager in search thereof: say: 'The knowledge thereof is with God (alone), but most men know not.' "
> (*al-A'rāf* 7:187)

There are many *Āyāt* and *Aḥādīth* concerning this subject:

Allah SWT said:

> "The Hour (of Judgement) is nigh, and the moon is cleft asunder."
> (*al-Qamar* 54:1)

The Prophet (S) said, whilst pointing with his index and middle fingers, "The time of my advent and the Hour are like these two fingers."[1] In another report he said, "The Hour almost came before me."

This indicates how close we are, relatively speaking, to the Hour.

Allah SWT said:

> "Closer and closer to mankind comes their Reckoning: yet they heed not and they turn away." (*al-Anbiyā'* 21:1)
>
> "(Inevitable) cometh (to pass) the Command of God: seek, ye not then to hasten it . . ." (*al-Naḥl* 16:1)
>
> "Only those wish to hasten it who believe not in it: those who believe hold it in awe, and know that it is the Truth . . ." (*al-Shūrā* 42:18)

In *Ṣaḥīḥ al-Bukhārī*, there is a *Ḥadīth* which states that a Bedouin asked the Prophet (S) about the Hour. He said, "It will surely come to pass. What have you prepared for it?" The man said, "O Messenger of Allah, I have not prepared much in the way of prayer and good works, but I love Allah and His Messenger." The Prophet (S) said, "You will be with those you love." The Muslims had never rejoiced as much as they did when they heard this *Ḥadīth*.[2]

Some *Aḥādīth* report that the Prophet (S) was asked about the Hour. He looked towards a young boy and said, "If he lives, he will not grow very old before he sees your Last Hour coming to you."[3] By this he meant their death and entering the Hereafter, because everyone who dies enters the Hereafter; some people say that when a person has died, his judgement has begun. This *Ḥadīth* with this meaning is "correct" (*Ṣaḥīḥ*).

Some heretics comment on this *Ḥadīth* and give it an incorrect meaning. The exact timing of the Great Hour (*al-Sā'at al-'Uẓmā*) is something which Allah alone knows and which He has not revealed to anyone, as is clear from the *Ḥadīth* in which the Prophet (S) said: "There are five things which nobody knows except Allah;" then he recited, "Verily the knowledge of the Hour is with God (alone). It is He Who sends down rain, and He Who knows what is in the wombs. Nor does anyone know what it is that he will earn on the morrow: nor does anyone know in what land he is to die. Verily with God is full knowledge and He is acquainted (with all things)."
(*Luqmān* 31:34)[4]

When Gabriel (AS) came to the Prophet (S) in the guise of a Bedouin, he asked him about *Islām, Īmān* (faith) and *Iḥsān* (excellence of faith), and the Prophet (S) answered his questions. But when he asked him about the Hour, he (S) said, "The one questioned about it knows no better than the questioner." Gabriel said, "Tell me about its signs." Then the Prophet (S) described them, as we shall see later when we quote this *Ḥadīth* and others in full.[5]

Ḥudhayfah said: "The Prophet (S) stood up one day to speak to us, and told us everything that was going to happen until the Hour, and left nothing unsaid. Some of the listeners learnt it by heart, and some forgot it; these friends of mine learnt it. I do not remember it completely, but sometimes it springs to mind, just as one might remember and recognize the face of a man whom one had forgotten, when one sees him." (Abū Dāwūd, Muslim.)[6]

Imām Aḥmad reported via Abū Nuḍrah that Abū Sa'īd said: "One day the Prophet (S) led us in praying the afternoon prayer (*Ṣalāt al-'Aṣr*). Then he stood and addressed us until sunset. He mentioned everything that was to happen until the Day of Resurrection, and left nothing unsaid. Some of us remembered it, and some of us forgot it. One of the things he said was: 'O people, this world is full of attractive temptations. Allah has appointed you as vicegerents (*Khalīfah*) in this world, and He will see how you will act. So guard yourselves against the temptations of this world and of women.' Towards the end of this speech, he said, 'The sun is about to set, and what remains of this world, compared to what has passed, is like what remains of this day compared to what has passed.' "[7]

'Alī ibn Zayd ibn Jad'ān al-Tīmī narrated some *Gharīb* and *Munkar Aḥadīth* – which could bring into question the validity of this *Ḥadīth*. But there are some reports which are similar to this *Ḥadīth*, and which were transmitted with different *isnāds*. Part of this *Ḥadīth* is reported in *Ṣaḥīḥ Muslim*, through Abū Nuḍrah on the authority of Abū Sa'īd. This *Ḥadīth* refers to something which is beyond any doubt: what remains of this world, compared to what has passed, is very little. In spite of that, no-one can know exactly how much time is left except Allah SWT, and no-one can know exactly how much time has passed, except Allah.

**FOOTNOTES.**

1. Bukhārī, *Kitāb al-Tafsīr*, commentary on *Sūrat al-Nāzi'ah*, 6/206.
2. A similar *Ḥadīth* was narrated by Bukhārī in *Kitāb al-Adab*.
3. See Bukhārī, *Kitāb al-Ādāb*; Muslim, *Kitāb al-Fitan wa Ashrāṭ al-Sā'ah*.
4. Bukhārī, *Kitāb al-Tafsīr*, commentary on *Luqmān* 31:34. A longer *Ḥadīth* is narrated by Muslim in *Kitāb al-Īmān*.
5. See page 10.
6. Muslim, *Kitāb al-Fitan wa Ashrāṭ al-Sā'ah*; Abū Dāwūd, *Kitāb al-Fitan wa 'l-Malāḥim*.
7. The whole speech is narrated by Imām Aḥmad in his *Musnad*, 2/61.

Chapter 2

# GENERAL DESCRIPTION OF THE FITAN (TRIBULATIONS).

Ḥudhayfah ibn al-Yamān said, "People used to ask the Prophet (S) about good things, but I used to ask him about bad things because I was afraid that they might overtake me. I said, 'O Messenger of Allah, we were lost in ignorance (*Jāhiliyyah*) and evil, then Allah brought this good (i.e. Islam). Will some evil come after this good thing?' He said, 'Yes'. I asked, 'And will some good come after that evil?' He said, 'Yes, but it will be tainted with some evil.' I asked, 'How will it be tainted?' He said, 'There will be some people who will lead others on a path different from mine. You will see good and bad in them.' I asked, 'Will some evil come after that good?' He said, 'Some people will be standing and calling at the gates of Hell; whoever responds to their call, they will throw him into the Fire.' I said, 'O Messenger of Allah, describe them for us.' He said, 'They will be from our own people, and will speak our language.' I asked, 'What do you advise me to do if I should live to see that?' He said, 'Stick to the main body (*jamā'ah*) of the Muslims and their leader (*Imām*).' I asked, 'What if there is no main body and no leader?' He said, 'Isolate yourself from all of these sects, even if you have to eat the roots of trees until death overcomes you while you are in that state.' "[1]

'Abd Allah ibn Mas'ūd said: "The Prophet (S) said, 'Islam began as something strange, and it will revert to being strange as it was in the beginning, so good tidings for the strangers.' Someone asked, 'Who are the strangers?' He said, 'The ones who break away from their people (literally, 'tribes') for the sake of Islam.' " This *Ḥadīth* was narrated by Ibn Mājah on the authority of Anas and Abū Hurayrah.[2]

**FOOTNOTES.**

1. Bukhārī, *Kitāb al-Fitan*, 9/65.
2. Muslim, *Kitāb al-Īmān*, 1/90; Ibn Mājah, *Kitāb al-Fitan* (*Ḥadīth* 3988), 2/1320.

Chapter 3

# DIVISIONS WITHIN THE MAIN RELIGIOUS GROUPS

Abū Hurayrah reported that the Prophet (S) said: "The Jews have split into seventy-one sects, and my Ummah will divide into seventy-three."[1]

'Awf ibn Mālik reported that the Prophet (S) said: "The Jews split into seventy-one sects: one will enter Paradise and seventy will enter Hell. The Christians split into seventy-two sects: seventy-one will enter Hell and one will enter Paradise. By Him in Whose hand is my soul, my Ummah will split into seventy-three sects: one will enter Paradise and seventy-two will enter Hell." Someone asked, "O Messenger of Allah, who will they be?" He replied, "The main body of the Muslims (*al-Jamā'ah*)." 'Awf ibn Mālik is the only one who reported this *Ḥadīth*, and its *isnād* is acceptable.[2]

Anas ibn Mālik said, "I shall tell you a *Ḥadīth* which I heard from the Messenger of Allah (S), and which no-one will tell you after me. I heard him say, 'Among the signs of the Hour will be the disappearance of knowledge and the appearance of ignorance. Adultery will be prevalent and the drinking of wine will be common. The number of men will decrease and the number of women will increase until there will be fifty women to be looked after by one man.' " This *Ḥadīth* was reported in the two *Ṣaḥīḥs* from the *Ḥadīth* of 'Abd Rabbihi.[3]

'Abd Allāh said, "The Prophet (S) said, 'Just before the Hour, there will be days in which knowledge will disappear and ignorance will appear, and there will be much killing.' " (Ibn Mājah; also narrated by Bukhārī and Muslim, from the *Ḥadīth* of al-A'mash.)[4]

Ḥudhayfah ibn al-Yamān said, "The Prophet (S) said,

'Islam will become worn out like clothes are, until there will be no-one who knows what fasting, prayer, charity and rituals are. The Qur'ān will disappear in one night, and no *Āyah* will be left on earth. Some groups of old people will be left who will say, We heard our fathers saying *Lā ilāha illā Allāh*, so we repeat it.'" Ṣilah asked Ḥudhayfah, "What will saying *Lā ilāha illā Allāh* do for them when they do not know what prayer, fasting, ritual and charity are?" Ḥudhayfah ignored him; then Ṣilah repeated his question three times, and each time Ḥudhayfah ignored him. Finally he answered, "O Ṣilah, it will save them from Hell", and said it three times. (Ibn Mājah.)

This indicates that in the last days, knowledge will be taken from the people, and even the Qur'ān will disappear from the *Muṣḥafs* and from people's hearts. People will be left without knowledge. Only the old people will tell them that they used to hear people saying *Lā ilāha illā Allāh*; and they will repeat it to feel close to Allah SWT, so it will give them some blessing, even if they do not have any good deeds or beneficial knowledge.

Knowledge will be taken away from men and ignorance will increase during the last days, because Allah will abandon them. They will remain like this, and their ignorance and misguidance will increase until the end, as in the *Ḥadīth* of the Prophet (S): "The Hour will not come upon anyone who says, 'Allah, Allah'; it will only come upon the most evil of men."[5]

**FOOTNOTES.**

1. Ibn Mājah, *Kitāb al-Fitan* (*Ḥadīth* 3991), 2/1321.
2. Abū Dāwūd, *Kitāb al-Sunnah* (*Ḥadīth* 4572, 4573), 12/1340-2. "The main body of the Muslims (*al-Jamā'ah*) means the people of the Qur'ān, *Ḥadīth, Fiqh* and other sciences, who have agreed to follow the Traditions of the Prophet (S) in all circumstances without introducing any changes or imposing their own confused ideas.
3. A similar *Ḥadīth* was narrated by al-Bukhārī in *Kitāb al-'Ilm*, 1/30,31; and by Muslim.
4. Bukhārī, *Kitāb al-Fitan*, 9/61; Muslim, *Kitāb al-'Ilm*, 8/58.
5. The first part of it was related by Muslim in *Kitāb al-Īmān*, 1/91, and the second part in *Kitāb al-Fitan wa Ashrāṭ al-Sā'ah*, 8/208.

## Chapter 4

# THE EVILS WHICH WILL BEFALL THE MUSLIM *UMMAH* DURING THE LAST DAYS.

'Abd Allāh ibn 'Umar said, "The Prophet (S) came to us and said, 'O *Muhājirūn*, (emigrants from Makkah to al-Madīnah) you may be afflicted by five things; God forbid that you should live to see them. If fornication should become widespread, you should realize that this has never happened without new diseases befalling the people which their forebears never suffered. If people should begin to cheat in weighing out goods, you should realize that this has never happened without drought and famine befalling the people, and their rulers oppressing them. If people should withhold *Zakāt*, you should realize that this has never happened without the rain being stopped from falling; and were it not for the animals' sake, it would never rain again. If people should break their covenant with Allah and His Messenger, you should realize that this has never happened without Allah sending an enemy against them to take some of their possessions by force. If the leaders do not govern according to the Book of Allah, you should realize that this has never happened without Allah making them into groups and making them fight one another.' " (Ibn Mājah.)[1]

'Alī ibn Abī Ṭālib said, "The Prophet (S) said: 'If my *Ummah* bears fifteen traits, tribulation will befall it.' Someone asked, 'What are they, O Messenger of Allah?' He said, 'When any gain is shared out only among the rich, with no benefit to the poor; when a trust becomes a means of making a profit; when paying *Zakāt* becomes a burden; when a man obeys his wife and disobeys his mother; and treats his friend kindly whilst shunning his father; when voices are raised in the mosques; when the leader of a people is the worst of them; when people treat a man with respect because they fear some evil he may do; when much wine is drunk; when men wear silk; when female singers and musical instruments become popular; when the last ones of this *Ummah* curse the first ones – then let them expect a red wind, or the earth to swallow them, or to be transformed into animals.' " (Tirmidhī.)[2]

'Alī ibn Abī Ṭālib said, "The Prophet (S) led us in praying *Ṣalāt al-Fajr* (the morning prayer). When he had finished, a man called to him: 'When will the Hour be?' The Prophet (S) reprimanded him and said 'Be quiet!' After a while he raised his eyes to the sky and said, 'Glorified be the One Who raised it and is taking care of it.' Then he lowered his gaze to the earth and said, 'Glory be to the One Who has outspread it and has created it.' Then the Prophet (S) said, 'Where is the one who asked me about the Hour?' The man knelt down and said, 'I asked you.' The Prophet (S) said, 'The Hour will come when leaders are oppressors, when people believe in the stars and reject *al-Qadar* (the Divine Decree of destiny) when a trust becomes a way of making a profit, when people give to charity (*Ṣadaqah*) reluctantly, when adultery becomes wide-spread – when this happens, then your people will perish.' "[3]

'Imrān ibn Ḥuṣayn said, "The Prophet (S) said, 'Some people of this *Ummah* will be swallowed up by the earth, some will be transformed into animals, and some will be bombarded with stones.' One of the Muslims asked, 'When will that be, O Messenger of Allah?' He said, 'When singers and musical instruments will become popular, and much wine will be drunk.' "[4]

**FOOTNOTES.**

1. Narrated by Ibn Mājah, *Kitāb al-Fitan* (*Ḥadīth* 4019), 2/1332.
2. Tirmidhī, *Abwāb al-Fitan* (*Ḥadīth* 308), 6/4620-458.
3. al-Haythamī, *Kitāb al-Fitan*.
4. Narrated by al-Tirmidhī.

## Chapter 5

# THE GREATER SIGNS OF THE HOUR

After the lesser signs of the Hour appear and increase, mankind will have reached a stage of great suffering. Then the awaited Mahdī will appear; he is the first of the greater, and clear, signs of the Hour. There will be no doubt about his existence, but this will only be clear to the knowledgeable people. The Mahdī will rule until the False Messiah (*al-Masīkh al-Dajjāl*) appears, who will spread oppression and corruption. The only ones who will know him well and avoid his evil will be those who have great knowledge and *Īmān* (faith). The false Messiah will remain for a while, destroying mankind completely, and the earth will witness the greatest *Fitnah* (tribulation) in its history. Then the Messiah Jesus (AS) will descend, bringing justice from heaven. He will kill the Dajjāl, and there will be years of safety and security.

Then the appearance of *Ya'jūj* and *Ma'jūj* (Gog and Magog) will take mankind by surprise, and corruption will overtake them again. In answer to Jesus' faithful prayer to Allah SWT, they will die, and safety, security, justice and stability will return. This state of affairs will continue for some years, until the death of Jesus (AS).

The '*Ulamā*' differ concerning the order in which the other greater signs of the Hour will come about. They are:

* The destruction of the Ka'bah and the recovery of its treasure.
* The rising of the sun from the West.
* The emergence of the Beast from the earth.
* The smoke.
* A wind will take the souls of the believers.
* The Qur'ān will be taken up into heaven.

* A fire will drive the people to their last gathering place.
* The Trumpet will be sounded: at the first sound everyone will feel terror; at the second sound all will be struck down; at the last sound all will be resurrected.

Chapter 6

# THE MAHDĪ

The Mahdī will come at the end of time; he is one of the Rightly-Guided Caliphs and Imāms. He is not the "Mahdī" who is expected by the Shī'ah, who they claim will appear from a tunnel in Sāmarrā'. This claim of theirs has no basis in reality nor in any reliable source. They allege that his name is Muḥammad ibn al-Ḥasan ibn al-'Askarī, and that he went into the tunnel when he was five years old.

The matter we intend to discuss has been proven by *Aḥādīth* narrated from the Prophet (S): that the Mahdī will appear at the end of time. I believe that he will appear before Jesus the son of Mary comes down, as the *Aḥādīth* indicate.

Ḥajjāj said that he heard 'Alī say, "The Prophet (S) said, 'Even if there were only one day left for the world, Allah would send a man from among us to fill the world with justice, just as it had been filled with oppression and injustice.'" (Aḥmad.)[1]

'Alī said, "The Prophet (S) said, 'The Mahdī is one of us, from among the people of my household. In one night Allah will inspire him and prepare him to carry out his task successfully.'" (Aḥmad and Ibn Mājah.)[2]

'Alī said, whilst looking at his son al-Ḥasan, "This son of mine is a *Sayyid* (master), as the Prophet (S) named him. Among his descendants there will be man named after your Prophet (S). He will resemble him in behaviour but not in looks." Then he told them the *report* which mentions that the earth will be filled with justice. (Abū Dāwūd.)[3]

Abū Dāwūd devoted a chapter of his *Sunan* to the subject of the Mahdī. At the beginning of this chapter he quoted the *Ḥadīth* of Jābir ibn Samrah, in which the Prophet (S) said, "This religion will remain steadfast until twelve caliphs have ruled over you." (According to another report he said, "This religion will remain strong until twelve caliphs have ruled over you.") Jābir said, "The people cheered and shouted *Allāhu akbar!* Then the Prophet (S) whispered something. I asked my father 'What did he say?' My father said, 'He said, All of them will be from Quraysh.' " Another report says that when the Prophet (S) returned to his house, Quraysh came to him and asked, "What will happen after that?" He said, "Then there will be tribulation and killing."

Abū Dāwūd reported a *Ḥadīth* from 'Abd Allāh ibn Mas'ūd: "The Prophet (S) said, 'If there were only one day left for the world, that day would be lengthened until a man from among my descendants or from among the people of my household, was sent; his name will be the same as my name, and his father's name will be the same as my father's name. He will fill the earth with justice and fairness, just as it will have been filled with injustice and oppression. The world will not end until a man of my household, whose name is the same as mine, holds sway."[4]

'Abd Allāh said, "The Prophet (S) said, 'A man from my household, whose name is like mine, will take power.' " (Tirmidhī.) In another report, from Abū Hurayrah, the Prophet (S) said, "If there were only one day left for this world, Allah would lengthen it until he took power."[5]

Abū Sa'īd said, "The Prophet (S) said, 'The Mahdī will be one of my descendants; he will have a high forehead and a hooked nose. He will fill the earth with justice and fairness just as it was filled with injustice and oppression, and he will rule for seven years.' " (Abū Dāwūd.)[6]

Umm Salamah said, "I heard the Prophet (S) say, 'The Mahdī will be one of my descendants, from the children of Fāṭimah.' " (Abū Dāwūd.)[7]

Umm Salamah reported that the Prophet (S) said, "People will begin to differ after the death of a *Khalīfah*. A man from the people of Madīnah will flee to Makkah. Some of the people of Makkah will come to him and drag him out against his will; they will swear allegiance to him between *al-Rukn* and *al-Maqām*. An army will be sent against him from Syria; it will be swallowed up in the desert between Makkah and Madīnah. When the people see this, groups of people from Syria and Iraq will come and swear allegiance to him. Then a man from Quraysh whose mother is from Kalb will appear and send an army against them, and will defeat them; this will be known as the Battle of Kalb. Whoever does not witness the spoils of this battle will miss much! The Mahdī will distribute the wealth, and will rule the people according to the *Sunnah* of the Prophet (S). Then he will die, and the Muslims will pray for him." (Abū Dāwūd.)[8]

'Alī said, "The Prophet (S) said, 'A man named al-Ḥārith ibn Ḥirāth will come from Transoxania. His army will be led by a man named Manṣūr. He will pave the way for and establish the government of the family of Muḥammad, just as Quraysh established the government of the Messenger of Allah (S). Every believer will be obliged to support him.'" (Abū Dāwūd.)

'Abd Allāh ibn al-Ḥārith ibn Juz' al-Zubaydī said, "The Prophet (S) said, 'A people will come out of the East who will pave the way for the Mahdī.'" (Ibn Mājah.)[9]

'Abd Allāh said, "Whilst we were with the Prophet (S), some young men from Banū Hāshim approached us. When the Prophet (S) saw them, his eyes filled with tears and the colour of his face changed. I said, 'We can see something has changed in your face, and it upsets us.' The Prophet (S) said, 'We are the people of a Household for whom Allah has chosen the Hereafter rather than this world. The people of my Household (*Ahl al-Bayt*) will suffer a great deal after my death, and will be persecuted until a people carrying black banners will come out of the east. They will instruct the people to do good, but the people will refuse; they will fight until they are victorious, and the people do as they asked, but they will not accept it from them until they hand over power to a man from my household. Then the earth will be filled with fairness, just as it had been filled with injustice. If any of you live to see this, you should go to him even if you have to crawl across ice.' "[10]

This text refers to the rule of the Abbasids, as we have mentioned above in the text referring to the beginning of their rule in 132 AH. It also indicates that the Mahdī will appear after the Abbasids, and that he will be one of the *Ahl al-Bayt*, a descendant of Fāṭimah, the daughter of the Prophet (S), through Ḥasan, not Ḥusayn, as mentioned in the *Ḥadīth* from 'Alī ibn Abī Ṭālib; and Allah knows best.[11]

Thawbān said, "The Prophet (S) said, 'Three men will be killed at the place where your treasure is. Each of them will be the son of a *Khalīfah*, and none of them will get hold of the treasure. Then the black banners will come out of the East, and they will slaughter you in a way which has never been seen before.' Then he said something which I do not remember; then, 'If you see him, go and give him your allegiance, even if you have to crawl over ice, because he is the *Khalīfah* of Allah, the Mahdī.' " (Ibn Mājah.)[12]

The treasure referred to in this text is the treasure of the Ka'bah. Towards the end of time, three of the sons of the *Khalīfahs* will fight to get hold of it, until the Mahdī appears. He will appear from the East, not from the tunnel of Sāmarrā', as the Shī'ah claim; they believe that he is in this tunnel now, and they are waiting for him to emerge at the end of time. There is no evidence for it in any book or *Ṣaḥīḥ* tradition, and there is no benefit in believing this.

The truth of the matter is that the Mahdī whose coming is promised at the end of time will appear from the East, and people will swear allegiance to him at the Ka'bah, as some *Aḥādīth* indicate.

At the time of the Mahdī, there will be peace and prosperity, with abundant crops and wealth, strong rulers, and Islam will be well-established.

Abū Sa'īd said, "By Allah, every ruler we have had has been worse than the previous one, and every year has been worse than the year before, but I heard the Prophet (S) say, 'Among your rulers will be one who will give out wealth freely, without counting it. A man will come and ask him for money, and he will say "Take"; the man will spread his cloak out and the ruler will pour money into it.' The Prophet (S) spread out a thick cloak he had been wearing, to demonstrate the man's actions; then he gathered it up by its corners and said, 'Then the man will take it and leave.' " (Aḥmad.)[13]

**FOOTNOTES.**

1. Aḥmad, *al-Musnad*; similar *Ḥadīth* in Abū Dāwūd, *Kitāb Awwal al-Mahdī*.
2. Aḥmad, *al-Musnad* and Ibn Mājah, *Kitāb al-Fitan*.
3. See Abū Dāwūd, *Kitāb al-Mahdī*.
4. *op. cit.*
5. al-Tirmidhī, in his chapters dealing with *al-Fitan*.
6. Abū Dāwūd, *Kitāb al-Mahdī*.
7. *op. cit.*
8. *op. cit.*
9. Ibn Mājah, *Kitāb al-Fitan* (*Ḥadīth* 3088).
10. Ibn Mājah, *ibid.*, *Ḥadīth* 4082.
11. See *Ḥadīth* on page 20.
12. Narrated by Ibn Mājah, *op. cit.*, *Ḥadīth* 4084.
13. Aḥmad, *Musnad*, 3/98.

Chapter 7

# DIFFERENT KINDS OF *FITAN* (TRIBULATION)

Zaynab bint Jaḥsh said, "The Prophet (S) got up from his sleep; his face was flushed and he said, 'There is no god but Allah. Woe to the Arabs, for a great evil which is nearly approaching them. Today a gap has been made in the wall of Gog and Magog like this (Sufyān illustrated this by forming the number 90 or 100 with his fingers). Someone asked, 'Shall we be destroyed even though there are righteous people among us?' The Prophet (S) said, 'Yes, if evil increases.' " (Bukhārī.)[1]

Umm Salamah, the wife of the Prophet (S) said, "One night the Prophet (S) got up and said, '*Subḥān Allāh!* How many tribulations have come down tonight, and how many treasures have been disclosed! Go and wake the dwellers of these apartments (i.e. his wives) for prayer. A well-dressed soul in this world may be naked in the Hereafter.' " (Bukhārī.)[2]

Usāmah ibn Zayd said, "Once the Prophet (S) stood over one of the battlements of al-Madīnah and asked the people, 'Do you see what I see?' They said, 'No.' He said, 'I see afflictions falling upon your houses as raindrops fall.' " (Bukhārī, Muslim.)[3]

Abū Hurayrah (RA) said, "The Prophet (S) said, 'Time will pass rapidly, knowledge will decrease, miserliness will become widespread in people's hearts, afflictions will appear, and there will be much *Harj*.' The people asked, 'O Messenger of Allah, what is *Harj*?' He said, 'Killing, killing!' " (Bukhārī.)[4]

Al-Zubayr ibn 'Adī narrated, "We went to Anas ibn Mālik and complained about the wrong we were suffering at the hands of al-Ḥajjāj. Anas ibn Mālik said, 'Be patient, "For no time will come but that the time following it will be worse, until you meet your Lord." I heard the Prophet (S) say that.'" (Bukhārī.)

Abū Hurayrah said, "The Prophet (S) said, 'There will come a time of afflictions when one who sits will be better than one who stands; one who stands will be better than one who walks; and one who walks will be better than one who runs. Whoever exposes himself to these afflictions, they will destroy him. So whoever can find a place of protection or refuge from them, should take shelter in it.'" (Bukhārī and Muslim.)[5]

Ḥudhayfah said, "The Prophet (S) told us two *Ḥadīth*, one of which I have seen fulfilled, and I am waiting for the fulfilment of the other. The Prophet (S) told us that honesty came down into men's hearts (from Allah); then they learnt it from the Qur'ān, and then from the *Sunnah*. The Prophet (S) told us that honesty would be taken away. He said, 'Man will be overtaken by sleep, during which honesty will be taken away from his heart, and only its trace will remain, like traces of a dark spot. Then man will be overtaken by slumber again, during which honesty will decrease still further, until its trace will resemble a blister such as is caused when an ember is dropped onto one's foot: it swells, but there is nothing inside. People will be carrying on with their trade, but there will hardly be any trustworthy persons. People will say, There is an honest man in such-and-such a tribe. Later they will say about some man, What a wise, polite and strong man he is! – although he will not have faith even the size of a mustard-seed in his heart.' Indeed, there came a time when I did not mind dealing with any one of you, for if he were a Muslim his Islam would compel him to pay whatever he owed me, and if he were a Christian, the Muslim official would compel him to pay it. But now I do not deal with anyone except so-and-so and so-and-so." (Bukhārī.)[6]

Ibn 'Umar said, "The Prophet (S) stood beside the pulpit, facing the east, and said, 'Afflictions will verily emerge from here, where the top of Satan's head will appear.'" (Bukhārī.)[7]

Abū Harayrah said that he had heard the Prophet (S) say, "The Hour will not come until a man passes by someone's grave and says, 'Would that I were in his place!' " (Bukhārī.)[8]

Abū Hurayrah said, "I heard the Prophet (S) say, 'The Hour will not come until the buttocks of the women of Daws move whilst going around Dhū 'l-Khalaṣah.' " Dhū 'l-Khalaṣah was an idol worshipped by the tribe of Daws during the *Jāhiliyyah*. (*Ḥadīth* from Bukhārī.)[9]

Abū Hurayrah also said, "The Prophet (S) said, 'The Euphrates will disclose a golden treasure. Whoever is present at that time should not take anything of it.' "[10]

Abū Hurayrah said, "The Prophet (S) said, 'The Hour will not come before the Euphrates uncovers a mountain of gold, for which people will fight. Ninety-nine out of every hundred will die, but every one among them will say that perhaps he will be the one who will survive (and thus possess the gold).' " (Muslim.)[11]

Abū Hurayrah said, "The Prophet (S) said, 'The Hour will not come until the following events have come to pass: two large groups will fight one another, and there will be many casualties; they will both be following the same religious teaching. Nearly thirty Dajjāls will appear, each of them falsely claiming to be a Messenger from Allah. Knowledge will disappear, earthquakes will increase, time will pass quickly, afflictions will appear, and *Harj* (i.e. killing) will increase. Wealth will increase, so that a wealthy man will worry lest no-one accept his *Zakāt*, and when he offers it to anyone, that person will say, "I am not in need of it." People will compete in constructing high buildings. When a man passes by someone's grave, he will say, "Would that I were in his place!" The sun will rise from the West; when it rises and the people see it, they will believe, but,

> "No good will it do to a soul to believe in them then, if it believed not before nor earned righteousness through its faith . . . "
> [*al-An'ām* 6:158]

"The Hour will come suddenly: when a man has milked his she-camel and taken away the milk, but he will not have time to drink it; before a man repairing a tank for his livestock will be able to put water in it for his animals; and before a man who has raised a morsel of food to his mouth will be able to eat it." (Bukhārī.)[12]

Ḥudhayfah ibn al-Yamān said, "Of all the people, I know most about every tribulation which is going to happen between now and the Hour. This is not because the Prophet (S) told me something in confidence which he did not tell anyone else; it is because I was present among a group of people to whom he spoke about the tribulations (*al-Fitan*). The Prophet (S) mentioned three tribulations which would hardly spare anybody, and some which would be like storms in summer; some would be great and some would be small. Everyone who was present at that gathering has passed away, except me." (Muslim.)[13]

Abū Hurayrah said, "I heard the Prophet (S) say, 'If you live for a while, you will see people go out under the wrath of Allah and come back under His curse, and they will have in their hands whips like the tail of an ox.' " (Aḥmad, Muslim.)

Abū Hurayrah said, "The Prophet (S) said, 'There are two types among the people of Hell whom I have not yet seen. The first are people who have whips like the tails of oxen, with which they beat people, and the second are women who are naked in spite of being dressed; they will be led astray and will lead others astray, and their heads will look like camels' humps. These women will not enter Paradise; they will not even experience the faintest scent of it, even though the fragrance of Paradise can be perceived from such a great distance.' "[15]

Anas ibn Mālik said, "The Prophet (S) was asked, 'O Messenger of Allah, (what will happen) when we stop enjoining good and forbidding evil?' He said, 'When what happened to the Israelites happens among you: when fornication becomes widespread among your leaders, knowledge is in the hands of the lowest of you, and power passes into the hands of the least of you.' " (Ibn Mājah.)[16]

Abū Hurayrah said, "The Prophet (S) said, 'Woe to the Arabs from the great evil which is nearly approaching them: it will be like patches of dark night. A man will wake up as a believer, and be a *kāfir* (unbeliever) by nightfall. People will sell their religion for a small amount of worldly goods. The one who clings to his religion on that day will be as one who is grasping an ember – or thorns.' " (Aḥmad.)[17]

Abū Hurayrah said, "I heard the Prophet (S) saying to Thawbān, 'O Thawbān, what will you do when the nations call one another to invade you as people call one another to come and eat from one bowl?' Thawbān said, 'May my father and my mother be sacrificed for you, O Messenger of Allah! Is it because we are so few?' The Prophet (S) said, 'No, on that day you (Muslims) will be many, but Allah will put weakness (*wahn*) in your hearts.' The people asked, 'What is that weakness, O Messenger of Allah?' He said, 'It is love for this world and dislike of fighting.' " (Aḥmad.)[18]

The Prophet (S) said, "There will be a tribulation in which one who is sleeping will be better than one who is lying down, one who is lying will be better than one who is sitting, one who is sitting will be better than one who is standing, one who is standing will be better than one who is walking, one who is walking will be better than one who is riding, and one who is riding will be better than one who is running; all of their dead will be in Hell." The Companion of the Prophet (S) who narrated this *Ḥadīth* said, "O Messenger of Allah, when will that be?" He said, "That will be the days of *Harj*." He asked, "When will the days of *Harj* be?" The Prophet (S) said, "When a man will not trust the person to whom he is speaking." The Companion asked, "What do you advise me to do if I live to see that?" He said, "Restrain yourself, and go back to your place of residence." The

Companion then asked, "O Messenger of Allah, what should I do if someone enters my neighbourhood to attack me?" He said, "Go into your house." The Companion asked, "What if he enters my house?" He said, "Go into the place where you pray and do this – and he folded his arms, – and say 'My Lord is Allah', until you die."[19]

Abū Bakrah said, "The Prophet (S) said, 'There will be a tribulation during which one who is lying down will be better than one who is sitting, one who is sitting will be better than one who is standing, one who is standing will be better than one who is walking, and one who is walking will be better than one who is running.' Someone asked, 'O Messenger of Allah, what do you advise me to do?' He said, 'Whoever has camels, let him stay with them, and whoever has land, let him stay in his land.' Someone asked, 'What about someone who does not have anything like that?' He said, 'Then let him take his sword and strike its edge against a stone, then go as far away as possible.' " (Abū Dāwūd; similar *Ḥadīth* in Muslim.)[20]

At the time of the *Fitnah* of 'Uthmān ibn 'Affān's *Khilāfah* (Caliphate), Sa'd ibn Abī Waqqāṣ said, "I bear witness that the Prophet (S) said, 'There will come a tribulation during which one who sits will be better than one who stands, one who stands will be better than one who walks, and one who walks will be better than one who runs.' Someone asked, 'What do you advise if someone enters my house to kill me?' He said, 'Be like the son of Adam (i.e. resign yourself).' " (Muslim, Tirmidhī.)[21]

Abū Mūsā al-Ash'arī said, "The Prophet (S) said, 'Before the Hour comes, there will be a tribulation like patches of dark night. A man will get up a believer and go to sleep a *kāfir*, or will go to sleep a believer and get up a *kāfir*. The one who sits will be better than one who stands, and one who walks will be better than one who runs. Break your bows, cut their strings, and strike your swords against stones. If someone comes to kill any of you, then be like the better of the two sons of Adam.' " (Abū Dāwūd.)[22]

Abū Dharr said, "The Prophet (S) was riding a donkey and sat me behind him. He said, 'O Abū Dharr, if the people were suffering from such severe hunger that you could not even get up from your bed to go to the mosque, what would you do?' I said, 'Allah and His Messenger know best.' He said, 'Be decent and restrain yourself.' Then he said, 'O Abū Dharr, if the people were suffering from severe death (i.e. if a man were worth no more than a grave), what would you do? If the people were killing one another, until Ḥajarat al-Zayt (an area of Madīnah) were submerged in blood, what would you do?' I said, 'Allah and His Messenger know best.' He said, 'Stay in your house and lock the door.' I asked, 'What if I am not left alone?' He said, 'Then be one of them.' I said, 'Should I take up my sword?' He said, 'If you did that, you would be joining them in their activities. No – if you fear that the brightness of the shining sword will disturb you, then cover your face with part of your clothing, and let him carry his own sin and your sin.' " (Aḥmad.)[23]

'Abd Allāh ibn 'Amr said, "We were on a journey with the Prophet (S) . . . When the Prophet's (S) caller called for prayer, I went there. The Prophet (S) was addressing the people, saying: 'O people, it has been the duty of every Prophet before me to guide his people to whatever he knew was good for them, and to warn them against whatever he knew was bad for them, but this *Ummah* has its time of peace and security at the beginning; at the end of its existence it will suffer trials and tribulations, one after the other. Tribulation will come, and the believer will say, "This will finish me", but it will pass. Another tribulation will come, and he will say, "This is it", but it will pass, and a third will come and go likewise. Whoever wishes to be rescued from Hell, and enter Paradise, let him die believing in Allah and the Last Day, and treat the people as he himself wishes to be treated. If anyone gives allegiance to an Imām, then let him obey him if he can (or on one occasion he said: as much as you can).' "

'Abd al-Raḥmān (one of the narrators of this *Ḥadīth*) said, "When I heard that, I put my head between my knees and said, 'But your cousin Mu'āwiyah is ordering us to squander our wealth among ourselves in vanity, and to kill each other, although Allạh SWT has said, "O ye who believe! Squander not your wealth among yourselves in vanity . . ." ' (*al-Nisā'*.) 4:29

" 'Abd Allāh [another narrator] put his head in his hands and paused awhile, then he raised his head and said, 'Obey him in that which is obedience to Allah and disobey that which is disobedience to Allah.' I asked him, 'Did you hear that from the Prophet (S)?' he said, 'Yes, I heard it with my ears and understood it in my heart.' " (Aḥmad, Abū Dāwūd, al-Nasā'ī, Ibn Mājah.)[24]

'Abd Allāh ibn 'Amr said, "I heard the Prophet (S) say, 'If you see my *Ummah* fearing a tyrant so much that they dare not tell him that he is a tyrant, then there will be no hope for them.' " The Prophet (S) said, "Among my *Ummah*, some will be swallowed up by the earth, some bombarded with stones, and some transformed into animals." (Aḥmad.)[25]

**FOOTNOTES.**

1. Bukhārī, *Kitāb al-Fitan*.
2. Bukhārī, *Kitāb al-'Ilm*.
3. Bukhārī, *Kitāb al-Fitan*, 9/60; Muslim, *Bāb Nuzūl al-Fitan ka-Mawāqi' al-Qaṭar*, 8/168.
4. Bukhārī, *ibid*.
5. *op. cit.*, 9/64; Muslim, *Bāb Nazūl al-Fitan ka-Mawāqi' al-Qaṭar*.
6. Bukhārī, *op. cit.*, 9/66.
7. Bukhārī, *Kitāb Bid' al-Khalq*, 4/150.
8. Bukhārī, *Kitāb al-Fitan*, 9/73.
9. Bukhārī, *Kitāb al-Fitan*, 8/182.
   Daws: a tribe in Yemen. Dhū'l-Khalaṣah: a house full of idols – it is so called because they believed that whoever worshipped it or went around it would be purified (*khallaṣa*).

   This *Ḥadīth* means that the tribe of Daws will become apostates from Islam and will go back to idol worship; even their women will exert themselves in worshipping the idol and running around it, so that their flesh will quiver.

10. Bukhārī, *Kitāb al-Fitan*, 9/73.
11. Muslim, *Kitāb al-Fitan wa Ashrāṭ al-Sā'ah*, 8/174.
12. Bukhārī, *Kitāb al-Fitan*, 9/74.
13. Muslim, *Kitab al-Fitan wa Ashrāṭ al-Sā'ah*, 8/172.
14. Muslim, *Kitāb al-Jannah wa Ṣifat Na'īmihā wa Ahlihā*, 8/155, 156.
    Aḥmad, *Musnad*, 2/308, 323, 5/250.
15. Muslim, *ibid.*
16. Ibn Mājah narrated a similar *Ḥadīth* in *Kitāb al-Fitan*, (*Ḥadīth* 4015), 2/1331.
    Aḥmad, *Musnad*, 3/187.
17. Aḥmad, *op. cit.*, 2/390.
18. *op. cit.*, 2/359.
19. *op. cit.*, 1/448.
20. Abū Dāwūd, *ibid.* (*Ḥadīth* 4236).
    Muslim, *Kitāb al-Fitan*, 8/169.
21. Tirmidhī, *Abwāb al-Fitan* (*Ḥadīth* 2290), 6/436, 438.
    Aḥmad, *Musnad*, 1/185.
22. Abū Dāwūd, *Kitāb al-Fitan wa'l-Malāḥim* (*Ḥadīth* 4139), 11/337.
23. Aḥmad, *Musnad*, 5/149; similar *Ḥadīth* in Abū Dāwūd, *Kitāb al-Fitan wa'l-Malāḥim* (*Ḥadīth* 4241), 11-340, 343.
24. Aḥmad, *Musnad*, 5/149. Muslim, *Kitāb al-Imārah*, 6-18. Ibn Mājah, *Kitāb al-Fitan* (*Ḥadīth* 3956), 2/1306, 1037. al-Nasā'ī, *Kitāb al-Bay'ah* (shorter version), 7 – 152, 153. Abū Dāwūd, *Kitāb al-Fitan* (shorter version), *Ḥadīth* 4229, 11 – 319.
25. Aḥmad, *Musnad*, 2/163.

## Chapter 8

# THE SIGNS AND PORTENTS OF THE HOUR

'Abd Allāh ibn 'Amr said, "I went to the Prophet (S) one day whilst he was performing *Wuḍū'* (ablution) slowly and carefully. He raised his head, looked at me and said, 'Six things will happen to this *Ummah*: the death of your Prophet – 'and when I heard that I was aghast,' – this is the first. The second is that your wealth will increase so much that if a man were given ten thousand, he would still not be content with it. The third is that tribulation will enter the house of every one of you. The fourth is that sudden death will be widespread. The fifth is a peace-treaty between you and the Romans; they will gather troops against you for nine months – like a woman's period of childbearing – then they will be the first to break the treaty. The sixth is the conquest of a city.' I asked, 'O Messenger of Allah, which city?' He said, 'Constantinople.'" (Aḥmad.)[1]

Abū Hurayrah said, "The Prophet (S) said, 'Hasten to do good deeds before six things happen: the rising of the sun from the West, the smoke, the Dajjāl, the beast, the (death) of one of you, or general tribulation.'" (Aḥmad, Muslim.)[2]

Ḥudhayfah ibn 'Ubayd said, "The Prophet (S) came upon us whilst we were busy in discussion. He asked us, 'What are you talking about?' We said, 'We are discussing the Hour.' He said, 'It will not come until you see ten signs: the smoke, the Dajjāl, the beast, the sun rising from the West, the descent of Jesus son of Mary, Gog and Magog, and three land-slides – one in the East, one in the West, and one in Arabia, at the end of which fire will burst forth from the direction of

Aden (Yemen) and drive people to the place of their final assembly.' " (Aḥmad.)[3]

**FOOTNOTES.**

1. Aḥmad, *Musnad*, 2/174.
2. Muslim, *Kitāb al-Fitan*, 8/207.
   Aḥmad, *Musnad*, 2/337, 372.
3. Muslim, *Kitāb al-Fitan*, 8/179.

## Chapter 9

# THE BATTLE WITH THE ROMANS

After the battle with the Romans, which ended with the conquest of Constantinople, the Dajjāl will appear, and Jesus son of Mary will descend from Heaven to the earth, to the white minaret in the east of Damascus, at the time of *Ṣalāt al-Fajr* (the morning prayer), as we shall see in the *Ṣaḥīḥ* Traditions.

Dhū Mukhammar said, "The Prophet (S) said, 'You will make a peace-treaty with the Romans, and together you will invade an enemy beyond Rome. You will be victorious and take much booty. Then you will camp in a hilly pasture; one of the Roman men will come and raise a cross and say "Victory to the Cross", so one of the Muslims will come and kill him. Then the Romans will break the treaty, and there will be a battle. They will gather an army against you and come against you with eighty banners, each banner followed by ten thousand men.'" (Aḥmad, Abū Dāwūd, Ibn Mājah.)[1]

Yusayr ibn Jābir said, "Once there was a red storm in Kūfah. A man came who had nothing to say except, 'O 'Abd Allāh ibn Mas'ūd, has the Hour come?' 'Abd Allāh was sitting reclining against something, and said, 'The Hour will not come until people will not divide inheritance, nor rejoice over booty.' Pointing towards Syria, he said, 'An enemy will gather forces against the Muslims and the Muslims will gather forces against them.' I asked, 'Do you mean the Romans?' He said, 'Yes. At that time there will be very heavy fighting. The Muslims will prepare a detachment to fight to the death; they will not return unless they are victorious. They will fight until night intervenes. Both sides will return without being victorious; then many will be killed on both sides. On the fourth day, the Muslims who are left will return to the fight, and Allah will cause the enemy to be routed. There will be a battle the like of which has never been seen, so that even if a bird were to pass their ranks, it would fall down dead before it reached the end of them. Out of a family of one hundred, only one man will survive, so how could he enjoy the booty or divide any inheritance? While they are in this state, they will hear of an even worse calamity. A cry will reach them: "The Dajjāl has taken your place among your offspring." So they will throw away whatever is in their hands and go forward, sending ten horsemen as a scouting party. The Prophet (S) said, 'I know their names, and the names of their fathers, and the colours of their horses. They will be the best horsemen on the face of the earth on that day.'" (Aḥmad, Muslim.)[2]

Abū Hurayrah said, "The Prophet (S) said, 'The Hour will not come until the Romans camp at al-A'mash or Dabīq. An army, composed of the best people on earth at that time, will come out from Madīnah to meet them. When they have arranged themselves in ranks, the Romans will say, 'Do not stand between us and those who took prisoners from amongst us. Let us fight with them.' The Muslims will say, 'No, by Allah, we will never stand aside from you and our brothers.' Then they will fight. One-third will run away, and Allah will never forgive them. One-third will be killed, and they will be the best of martyrs in Allah's sight. One-third, who will never be subjected to trials or tribulations, will win, and will conquer Constantinople. Whilst they are sharing out the booty, after hanging their swords on the olive-trees, Satan will shout to them that the Dajjāl has taken their place among their families. They will rush out, but will find that it is not true. When they come to Syria, the Dajjāl will appear, while they are preparing for battle and drawing up the ranks. When the time for prayer comes, Jesus the son of Mary will descend and lead them in prayer. When the enemy of Allah (i.e. the Dajjāl) sees him, he will start to dissolve like salt in water, but Allah will kill him.' " (Muslim.)[3]

The Prophet (S) said, "The Hour will not come until the furthest border of the Muslims will be in Bulā." Then he said, "O 'Alī!" 'Alī said, "May my father and mother be sacrificed for you!" The Prophet (S) said, "You will fight the Romans, and those who come after you will fight them, until the best people among the Muslims, the people of al-Ḥijāz, will go out to fight them, fearing nothing but Allah. They will conquer Constantinople with *Tasbīḥ* and *Takbīr* (saying "*Subḥān Allāh*" and "*Allāhu Akbar*"), and they will obtain booty the like of which has never been seen – they will share it out by scooping it up with their shields. Someone will come and say, 'The Dajjāl has appeared in your land', but he will be lying. Anyone who takes notice of him will regret it, and anyone who ignores him will regret it." (Ibn Mājah.)[4]

Nāfi' ibn 'Utbah said, "The Prophet (S) said, 'You will attack Arabia, and Allah will enable you to conquer it. Then you will attack Persia, and Allah will enable you to conquer it. Then you will attack Rome, and Allah will enable you to conquer it. Then you will attack the Dajjāl, and Allah will enable you to conquer him.' " (Muslim.)[5]

When Mustawrid al-Qurashī was sitting with 'Amr ibn al-'Āṣ, he said, "I heard the Prophet (S) say, 'The Hour will come when the Romans will be in the majority.' 'Amr asked him, "What are you saying?" He said, "I am repeating that which I heard from the Prophet (S)." 'Amr said, "If you say this, it is true, because they have four good characteristics: they are the most able to cope with tribulation, the quickest to recover after disaster and to return to the fight after disaster, and are the best as far as treating the poor, weak and orphans is concerned. They have a fifth characteristic which is very good: they do not allow themselves to be oppressed by their kings."[6]

The Prophet (S) said, "You will fight the Romans, and Believers from the Ḥijāz will fight them after you, until Allah enables them to conquer Constantinople and

Rome with *Tasbīḥ* and *Takbīr* (saying "*Subḥān Allāh*" and "*Allāhu Akbar*"). Its fortifications will collapse, and they will obtain booty the like of which has never been seen, so that they will share it out by scooping it up with their shields. Then someone will cry, 'O Muslims! the Dajjāl is in your country, with your families', and the people will leave the wealth. Anyone who takes notice will regret it and anyone who ignores it will regret it. They will ask, 'Who shouted?' but they will not know who he is. They will say, 'Send a vanguard to Ilyā'. If the Dajjāl has appeared, you will hear about his deeds.' So they will go and see, and if they see that everything is normal, they will say, 'No-one would give a shout like that for no reason, so let us go together to Ilyā'.' If we find the Dajjāl there we will fight him together, until Allah decides between us and him. If we do not find the Dajjāl, we will go back to our country and our families.' "[7]

Mu'ādh ibn Jabal said, "The Prophet (S) said, 'The building of Bayt al-Maqdis (in Jerusalem) will be followed by the destruction of Yathrib (Madīnah), which will be followed by a fierce battle, which will be followed by the conquest of Constantinople, which will be followed by the appearance of the Dajjāl.' Then he put his hand on the thigh or the shoulder of the one with whom he was speaking (i.e. Mu'ādh), and said, 'This is as true as the fact that you are here (or as true as you are sitting here).' "

This does not mean that Madīnah will be destroyed completely before the appearance of the Dajjāl, but that will happen at the end of time, as we shall see in some authentic *Aḥādīth*. But the building of Bayt al-Maqdis will be the cause of the destruction of Madīnah, as it was proven in the *Ḥadīth* that the Dajjāl will not be able to enter Madīnah. He will be prevented from doing so because it is surrounded by angels bearing unsheathed swords.[8]

Abū Hurayrah said, "The Prophet (S) said about Madīnah: 'Neither plague nor the Dajjāl can enter it.' " (Bukhārī.)[9]

**FOOTNOTES.**

1. Similar *Ḥadīth* in Abū Dāwūd, *Kitāb al-Malāḥim*, (*Ḥadīth* 4271), 11/397/399.
   Ibn Mājah, *Kitāb al-Fitan* (*Ḥadīth* 4089), 2/1369.
   Aḥmad, *Musnad*, 9104.
2. Muslim, *Kitāb al-Fitan*, 8/177, 178.
   Aḥmad, *Musnad*, 1/384, 385.
3. Muslim, *Kitāb al-Fitan*, 8 – 175, 176. Al-A'mash is a place outside the city, and Dabīq is a market-place in the city. "The city" refers to Aleppo (some say Damascus).
4. Ibn Mājah, *Kitāb al-Fitan* (*Ḥadīth* 4094), 2 – 1370.
   The one who believes the liar will regret it, because he will find that the Dajjāl is not there. The one who does not believe him will regret it because the Dajjāl will appear soon afterwards.
5. Muslim, *Kitāb al-Fitan wa Ashrāṭ al-Sā'ah*, 8 – 178.
   Ibn Mājah, *Bāb al-Malāḥim* (*Ḥadīth* 4091), 2 – 1380.
6. Muslim, *Kitāb al-Fitan*, 8 – 176.
7. Al-Haythamī, *Majma' al-zawā'id*.
   Ibn Mājah, 7:248.
8. Abū Dāwūd, *Kitāb al-Malāḥim* (*Ḥadīth* 4273), 11 – 400, 401; Aḥmad, *Musnad*, 5/245.
   "The building of Bayt al-Maqdis" – i.e., after the *kuffār* (unbelievers) have destroyed it, the Muslims will rebuild it.
9. Bukhārī, *Kitāb al-Fitan*, 9/76.

Chapter 10

# THE APPEARANCE OF THE DAJJĀL

First of all, we will quote the reports which mention the liars and "dajjāls" who will precede the coming of the Dajjāl, or Antichrist, who will be the last of them; may Allah curse them and punish them with Hell-fire.

Jābir ibn Samūrah said, "I heard the Prophet (S) say, 'Just before the Hour there will be many liars.' " Jābir said, "Be on your guard against them." (Muslim.)[1]

Jābir said, "I heard the Prophet (S) say, 'Just before the Hour there will be many liars; among them is the one in al-Yamāmah, the 'Ansī in San'ā', the one in Ḥimyar, and the Dajjāl. This will be the greatest *fitnah*.' " (Aḥmad.)[2]

Abū Hurayrah said, "The Prophet (S) said, 'The Hour will not come . . . until nearly thirty "dajjāls" (liars) appear, each one claiming to be a messenger from Allah.' " (Bukhārī, Muslim.)[3]

Abū Hurayrah said, "The Prophet (S) said, 'The Hour will not come until thirty "dajjāls" appear, each of them claiming to be a messenger from Allah, wealth increases, tribulations appear and *al-Harj* increases.' " Someone asked, 'What is *al-Harj*?' He said, 'Killing, killing.' (Aḥmad.)[4]

Abū Hurayrah said, "The Prophet (S) said, 'The Hour will not come until thirty "dajjāls" appear, all of them lying about Allah and His Messenger. " (Abū Dāwūd.)[5]

Abū Hurayrah said, "The Prophet (S) said, 'Just before the Hour, there will be thirty "dajjāls", each of whom will say, I am a Prophet.' " (Aḥmad.)[6]

Abū Hurayrah said, "The Prophet (S) said, 'There will be "dajjāls" and liars among my *Ummah*. They will tell you something new, which neither you nor your forefathers have heard. Be on your guard against them, and do not let them lead you astray.' " (Aḥmad.)[7]

Thawbān said, "The Prophet (S) said, 'There will be thirty liars among my *Ummah*. Each one will claim that he is a prophet; but I am the last of the Prophets (Seal of the Prophets), and there will be no Prophet after me.' " (Aḥmad.)[8]

The Prophet (S) said, "Verily before the Day of Resurrection there will appear the Dajjāl, and thirty or more liars." (Aḥmad.)[9]

Ibn 'Umar said, "I heard the Prophet (S) say, 'Among my *Ummah* there will be more than seventy callers, each of whom will be calling people to Hell-fire. If I wished, I could tell you their names and tribes.' "

Abū Bakrah said, "The people spoke a great deal against Musaylimah before the Prophet (S) said anything about him. Then the Prophet (S) got up to give a speech and said: '. . . as for this man about whom you have spoken so much – he is one of the thirty liars who will appear before the Hour, and there is no town which will not feel the fear of the Antichrist.' " (Aḥmad.)[10]

In another version of this report, the Prophet (S) said, "He is one of the thirty liars who will appear before the Dajjāl. There is no town which will escape the fear of the Dajjāl, apart from Madīnah. At that time there will be two angels at every entrance of Madīnah, warding off the fear of the Antichrist."[11]

Anas ibn Mālik said, "The Prophet (S) said, 'The time of the Dajjāl will be years of confusion. People will believe a liar, and disbelieve one who tells the truth. People will distrust one who is trustworthy, and trust one who is treacherous; and the *Ruwaybiḍah* will have a say.' Someone asked, 'Who are the *Ruwaybiḍah*?' He said, 'Those who rebel against Allah and will have a say in general affairs.' " (Aḥmad.)[12]

**FOOTNOTES.**

1. Muslim, *Kitāb al-Fitan*, 8/189.
2. Aḥmad, *Musnad*, 3/345.
3. See page 27, where the *Ḥadīth* is quoted in full.
4. Aḥmad, *Musnad*, 2 – 457.
5. *op. cit.,* 2/450.
6. *op. cit.,* 2/429.
7. *op. cit.,* 20/349.
8. *op. cit.,* 5/46.
9. *op. cit.,* 2/95.
10. *op. cit.,* 5/41, 46.
11. *op. cit.,* 5/46.
12. *op. cit.,* 3/220.

Chapter 11

# AḤĀDĪTH ABOUT THE DAJJĀL

'Abd Allāh ibn 'Umar said, " 'Umar ibn al-Khaṭṭāb went along with the Prophet (S) and a group of people to Ibn Ṣayyād, and found him playing with some children near the battlement of Banū Maghālah. At that time Ibn Ṣayyād was on the threshold of adolescence; he did not realise that anybody was near until the Prophet (S) struck him on the back. The Prophet (S) said to him: 'Do you bear witness than I am the Messenger of Allah?' Ibn Ṣayyād looked at him and said, 'I bear witness that you are the Prophet of the unlettered.' Then Ibn Ṣayyād said to the Prophet (S), 'Do you bear witness that I am the Messenger of Allah?' The Prophet (S) dismissed this and said, 'I believe in Allah and His Messengers.' Then the Prophet (S) asked him, 'What do you see?' Ibn Ṣayyād said, 'Sometimes a truthful person comes to me, and sometimes a liar.' The Prophet (S) said to him, 'You are confused', then he said, 'I am hiding something from you.' Ibn Ṣayyād said, 'It is *Dukh*.' The Prophet (S) said, 'Silence! You will not be able to go beyond your rank.' 'Umar ibn al-Khaṭṭāb said, 'O Messenger of Allah, shall I cut off his head?' The Prophet (S) said, 'If he is [the *Dajjāl*], you will not be able to overpower him, and if he is not, then killing will not do you any good.' "

Sālim ibn 'Abd Allāh said, "I heard 'Abd Allāh ibn 'Umar say, 'After that, the Prophet (S) and Ubayy ibn Ka'b went along to the palm trees where Ibn Ṣayyād was. The Prophet (S) started to hide behind a tree, with the intention of hearing something from Ibn Ṣayyād before Ibn Ṣayyād saw him. The Prophet (S) saw him lying on a bed, murmuring beneath a blanket. Ibn Ṣayyād's mother saw the Prophet (S) hiding behind a tree, and said to her son, "O Ṣāf [Ibn Ṣayyād's first name], here is Muḥammad!" Ibn Ṣayyād jumped up, and the Prophet (S) said, "If you had left him alone, he would have explained himself." '

Sālim said, "Abd Allāh ibn 'Umar said, The Prophet (S) stood up to address the people. He praised Allah SWT as He deserved to be praised, then he spoke about the Dajjāl: 'I warn you against him; there is no Prophet who has not warned his people against him – even Noah warned his people against him. But I will tell you something which no other Prophet has told his people. You must know that the Dajjāl is one-eyed, and Allah is not one-eyed.' "

Ibn Shihāb said, " 'Umar ibn Thābit al-Anṣārī told me that some of the Companions of the Prophet (S) told him that on the day when he warned the people about the Dajjāl, the Prophet (S) said, 'There will be written between his eyes the word *Kāfir* (unbeliever). Everyone who resents his bad deeds – or every believer – will be able to read it.' He also said, 'You must know that no one of you will be able to see his Lord until he dies.' " (Muslim, Bukhārī.)[1]

Ibn 'Umar said, "The Prophet (S) mentioned the Dajjāl to the people. He said, 'Allah SWT is not one-eyed, but the Dajjāl is blind in his right eye, and his eye is like a floating grape.' " (Muslim.)[2]

Anas ibn Mālik said, "The Prophet (S) said, 'there has never been a Prophet who did not warn his people against that one-eyed liar. Verily he is one-eyed and your Lord is not one-eyed. On his forehead will be written the letters *Kāf, Fā', Rā' (Kāfir).*' " (Muslim, Bukhārī.)[3]

Ḥudhayfah said, "The Prophet (S) said, 'I know more about the powers which the Dajjāl will have than he will know himself. He will have two flowing rivers: one will appear to be pure water, and the other will appear to be flaming fire. Whosoever lives to see that, let him choose the river which seems to be fire, then let him close his eyes, lower his head and drink from it, for it will be cold water. The Dajjāl will be one-eyed; the place where one eye should be will be covered by a piece of skin. On his forehead will be written the word *Kāfir*, and every believer, whether literate or illiterate, will be able to read it.' " (Muslim.)[4]

Abū Hurayrah said, "The Prophet (S) said, 'Shall I tell you something about the Dajjāl which no Prophet has ever told his people before me? The Dajjāl is one-eyed and will bring with him something which will resemble Paradise and Hell; but that which he calls Paradise will in fact be Hell. I warn you against him as Noah warned his people against him.' " (Bukhārī, Muslim.)[5]

Muḥammad ibn Munkadir said, "I saw Jābir ibn 'Abd Allāh swearing by Allah that Ibn Ṣayyād was the Dajjāl, so I asked him, 'Do you swear by Allah?' He said, 'I heard 'Umar swear to that effect in the presence of the Prophet (S), and the Prophet (S) did not disapprove of it.' "[6]

Some *'ulamā'* (scholars) say that some of the *Ṣaḥābah* (Companions of the Prophet) believed Ibn Ṣayyād to be the greater Dajjāl, but that is not the case: Ibn Ṣayyād was a lesser dajjāl.

Ibn Ṣayyād travelled between Makkah and Madīnah with Abū Sa'īd, and complained to him about the way that people were saying that he was the Dajjāl. Then he said to Abū Sa'īd, "Did not the Prophet say that the Dajjāl would not enter Madīnah? – I was born there. Did not he say that he would not have any children? – I have children. Did not he say that he would be a *Kāfir*? – I have embraced Islam. Of all the people, I know the most about him: I know where he is now. If I were given the opportunity to be in his place, I would not resent it.' " (Bukhārī, Muslim.)

There are many *Aḥādīth* about Ibn Ṣayyād, some of which are not clear as to whether he was the Dajjāl or not. We shall see *Aḥādīth* which indicates that the Dajjāl is not Ibn Ṣayyād, as in the *Ḥadīth* of Fāṭimah Bint Qays al-Fahriyyah, although this does not mean that he was not one of the lesser Dajjāl; but Allah knows best.

**FOOTNOTES.**

1. Bukhārī, *Kitāb al-Adab*, 8/49, 50.
   Muslim, *Kitāb al-Fitan*, 8/192, 193.
   Ibn Ṣayyād's [or Ibn Ṣa'īd's] first name was Ṣāf.
   He had some characteristics similar to those ascribed to the Dajjāl. When he was young, he was like a *Kāhin* (soothsayer) – sometimes he spoke the truth, sometimes he lied. When he grew up, he embraced Islam and displayed some good characteristics, but later he changed, and it was said that his behaviour might indicate that he was the Dajjāl. But the Prophet (S) had not received any *Waḥy* (revelation) to that effect, so he told 'Umar: "If he is [the Dajjāl] you will not be able to overpower him."
   – Banū Maghālah: if you stand facing the Masjid al-Nabawī, (the Prophet's Mosque in Madīnah), everything on your right is the territory of Banū Maghālah.
   – *Dukh*: i.e. *al-Dukhān* (smoke). The Prophet (S) was thinking of the *Āyah*, "Then watch thou for the Day that the sky will bring forth a kind of smoke (or mist) plainly visible." (*al-Dukhān* 44:10.)
   – ". . . with the intention of hearing something . . . " in other words, the Prophet (S) wanted to eavesdrop on Ibn Ṣayyād so that he and his companions could find out whether he was a soothsayer (*kāhin*) or a sorcerer.
   – "if you had left him alone, he would have explained himself": i.e., if his mother had not told him that the Prophet (S) was there, then the Prophet (S) would have found out what he was – a soothsayer or a sorcerer.
2. Muslim, *Kitāb al-Fitan*, 8/194, 195.
   "His eye is like a floating grape" – this means that, his eye will protrude and there will be some kind of brightness in it.
3. Muslim, *ibid.*
   Bukhārī, *Kitāb al-Fitan*, 9/75, 76.
   "On his forehead will be written the letters *Kāf, Fā', Rā'*" – this indicates that he will call people to *Kufr*, not the right path, so we must avoid him. The fact that Muslims will be able to identify him as a *Kāfir* is a great blessing from Allah to this *Ummah*.
4. Muslim, *ibid.*
   Shorter version in Bukhārī, *Kitāb al-Fitan*, 9/75.
5. Bukhārī, *Kitāb al-Anbiyā'*, 4/163.
   Muslim, *Kitāb al-Fitan*, 8/196.
6. Muslim, *Kitāb al-Fitan*, 8/192.

## Chapter 12

# THE *ḤADĪTH* OF FĀṬIMAH BINT QAYS

'Āmir ibn Sharāḥīl Sha'bi Sha'b Ḥamdān reported that he asked Fāṭimah bint Qays, the sister of Daḥḥāk ibn Qays, who was one of the first *Muhājirāt*, "Tell me a *Ḥadīth* which you heard directly from the Prophet (S), with no narrator in between." She said, "I can tell you if you like." He said, "Yes, please tell me." she said, "I married Ibn al-Mughīrah, who was one of the best of the youth of Quraysh in those days. But he fell in the first *Jihād* on the side of the Prophet (S).

"When I became a widow, 'Abd al-Raḥmān ibn 'Awf, one of the Companions of the Prophet (S), sent me a proposal of marriage. The Prophet (S) also sent me a proposal of marriage on behalf of his freedman Usāmah ibn Zayd. I had been told that the Prophet (S) had said, 'He who loves me should also love Usāmah.' When the Prophet (S) spoke to me, I said, 'It is up to you: marry me to whomever you wish.'

"The Prophet (S) said, 'Go and stay with Umm Sharīk.' Umm Sharīk was a rich Anṣārī (Muslim originally from Madīnah) woman, who spent much in the way of Allah and entertained many guests. I said, 'I will do as you wish.' Then he said, 'Don't go. Umm Sharīk has many guests, and I would not like it if your head or leg were to become uncovered accidentally and people saw something you would not wish them to see. It is better if you go and stay with your cousin 'Abd Allāh ibn 'Amr ibn Umm Maktūm' (Abd Allāh was of the Banū Fihr of Quraysh, the same tribe as that to which Fāṭimah belonged).

"So I went to stay with him, and when I had completed my *'Iddah* (period of waiting), I heard the

Prophet's (S) announcer calling for congregational prayer. I went out to the mosque, and prayed behind the Prophet (S). I was in the women's row, which was at the back of the congregation. When the Prophet (S) had finished his prayer, he sat on the pulpit, smiling, and said, 'Everyone should stay in his place.' Then he said, 'Do you know why I have asked you to assemble?' The people said, 'Allah and His Messenger know best.'

"He said, 'By Allah, I have not gathered you here to give you an exhortation or a warning. I have kept you here because Tamīm al-Dārī, a Christian man who has come and embraced Islam, told me something which agrees with that which I have told you about the Dajjāl. He told me that he had sailed in a ship with thirty men from Banū Lakhm and Banū Judhām. The waves had tossed them about for a month, then they were brought near to an island, at the time of sunset. They landed on the island, and were met by a beast who was so hairy that they could not tell its front from its back. They said, "Woe to you! What are you?" It said, "I am al-Jassāsah." They said, "What is al-Jassāsah?" It said, "O people, go to this man in the monastery, for he is very eager to know about you." Tamīm said that when it named a person to us, we were afraid lest it be a devil.

"Tamīm said, 'We quickly went to the monastery. There we found a huge man with his hands tied up to his neck and with iron shackles between his legs up to the ankles. We said, "Woe to you, who are you?" He said, "You will soon know about me. Tell me who you are." We said, "We are people from Arabia. We sailed in a ship, but the waves have been tossing us about for a month, and they brought us to your island, where we met a beast who was so hairy that we could not tell its front from its back. We said to it, "Woe to you! What are you?" and it said, "I am al-Jassāsah." We asked, "What is al-Jassāsah?" and it told us, "Go to this man in the monastery, for he is very eager to know about you." So we came to you quickly, fearing that it might be a devil.'

"The man said, 'Tell me about the date-palms of Baysān.' We said, 'What do you want to know about them?' He said, 'I want to know whether these trees bear fruit or not.' We said, 'Yes.' He said, 'Soon they will not bear fruit.' Then he said, 'Tell me about the lake of al-Ṭabariyyah [Tiberias, in Palestine].' We said, 'What do you want to know about it?' He asked, 'Is there water in it?' We said, 'There is plenty of water in it.' He said, 'Soon it will become dry.' Then he said, 'Tell me about the spring of Zughar.' We said, 'What do you want to know about it?' He said, 'Is there water in it, and does it irrigate the land?' We said, 'Yes, there is plenty of water in it, and the people use it to irrigate the land.'

"Then he said, 'Tell me about the unlettered Prophet – what has he done?' We said, 'He has left Makkah and settled in Yathrib.' He asked, 'Do the Arabs fight against him?' We said, 'Yes.' He said, 'How does he deal with them?' So we told him that the Prophet (S) had overcome the Arabs around him and that they had followed him. He asked, 'Has it really happened?' We said, 'Yes.' He said, 'It is better for them if they follow him. Now I will tell you about myself. I am the Dajjāl. I will soon be permitted to leave this place: I will emerge and travel about the earth. In forty nights I will pass through every town, except Makkah and Madīnah, for these have been forbidden to me. Every time I try to enter either of them, I will be met by an angel bearing an unsheathed sword, who will prevent me from entering. There will be angels guarding them at every passage leading to them.'

Fāṭimah said, "The Prophet (S), striking the pulpit with his staff, said: 'This is Ṭayyibah, this is Ṭayyibah, this is Ṭayyibah [i.e. Madīnah]. Have I not told you something like this?' The people said, 'Yes.' He said, 'I liked the account given to me by Tamīm because it agrees with that which I have told you about the Dajjāl, and about Makkah and Madīnah. Indeed he is in the Syrian sea or the Yemen sea. No, on the contrary, he is in the East, he is in the East, he is in the East' – and he pointed towards the East. Fāṭimah said: I memorized this from the Prophet (S)." (Muslim.)[1]

'Abd Allāh ibn 'Umar said, "The Prophet (S) said, 'While I was asleep, I saw myself in a dream performing *Ṭawāf* (circumambulation) around the *Ka'bah*. I saw a ruddy man with lank hair and water dripping from his head. I said, "Who is he?" and they said, "The son of Mary." Then I turned around and saw another man with a huge body, red complexion, curly hair and one eye. His other eye looked like a floating grape. They said, "This is the Dajjāl." The one who most resembles him is Ibn Qaṭan, a man from the tribe of al-Khuzā'ah.' " (Bukhārī, Muslim.)[2]

Jābir ibn 'Abd Allāh said, "The Prophet (S) said, 'The Dajjāl will appear at the end of time, when religion is taken lightly. He will have forty days in which to travel throughout the earth. One of these days will be like a year, another will be like a month, a third will be like a week, and the rest will be like normal days. He will be riding a donkey; the width between its ears will be forty cubits. He will say to the people: "I am your lord." He is one-eyed, but your Lord is not one-eyed. On his forehead will be written the word *Kāfir*, and every believer, literate or illiterate, will be able to read it. He will go everywhere except Makkah and Madīnah, which Allah has forbidden to him; angels stand at their gates. He will have a mountain of bread, and the people will face hardship, except for those who follow him. He will have two rivers, and I know what is in them. He will call one Paradise and one Hell. Whoever enters the one he calls Paradise will find that it is Hell, and whoever enters the one he calls Hell will find that it is Paradise. Allah will send with him devils who will speak to the people. He will bring a great tribulation; he will issue a command to the sky and it will seem to the people as if it is raining. Then he will appear to kill someone and bring him back to life. After that he will no longer have this power. The people will say, "Can anybody do something like this except the Lord?" The Muslims will flee to Jabal al-Dukhān in Syria, and the Dajjāl will come and besiege them. The siege will intensify and they will suffer great hardship. Then Jesus son of Mary will descend, and will call the people at dawn: "O people, what prevented you from coming out to fight this evil liar?" They will answer, "He is a *Jinn*." Then they will go out, and find Jesus son of Mary. The time for prayer will come, and the Muslims will call on Jesus to lead the prayer, but he will say, "Let your Imām lead the prayer." Their Imām will lead them in praying *Ṣalāt al-Ṣubḥ* (Morning prayer), then they will go out to fight the Dajjāl. When the liar sees Jesus, he will dissolve like salt in water. Jesus will go to him and kill him, and he will not let anyone who followed him live.' " (Aḥmad.)[3]

**FOOTNOTES.**

1. Muslim, *Kitāb al-Fitan*, 8/203-205.
   Al-Jassāsah is so called because he spies on behalf of the Dajjāl (from *jassa* – to try to gain information, to spy out, etc.).
   Baysān – a village in Palestine.
   'Ayn Zughar (the spring of Zughar) is a town in Palestine.
2. Bukhārī, *Kitāb al-Fitan*, 9/75.
   Muslim, *Kitāb al-Īmān*, 1/108.
3. Aḥmad, *Musnad*, 3/367, 368.

## Chapter 13

# THE *ḤADĪTH* OF AL-NUWĀS IBN SAM'ĀN AL-KILĀBĪ

Al-Nuwās ibn Sam'ān said, "One morning the Prophet (S) spoke about the Dajjāl. Sometimes he described him as insignificant, and sometimes he described him as so dangerous that we thought he was in the clump of date-palms nearby. When we went to him later on, he noticed that fear in our faces, and asked, 'What is the matter with you?' We said, 'O Messenger of Allah, this morning you spoke of the Dajjāl; sometimes you described him as insignificant, and sometimes you described him as being so dangerous that we thought he was in the clump of date-palms nearby.'

"The Prophet (S) said, 'I fear for you in other matters besides the Dajjāl. If he appears whilst I am among you, I will contend with him on your behalf. But if he appears while I am not among you, then each man must contend with him on his own behalf, and Allah will take care of every Muslim on my behalf. The Dajjāl will be a young man, with short, curly hair, and one eye floating. I would liken him to 'Abd al-'Uzzā ibn Qaṭan. Whoever amongst you lives to see him should recite the opening *Āyāt* of *Sūrat al-Kahf*. He will appear on the way between Syria and Iraq, and will create disaster left and right. O servants of Allah, adhere to the Path of Truth.' "

"We said, 'O Messenger of Allah, for the day which is like a year, will one day's prayers be sufficient?' He said, 'No, you must make an estimate of the time, and then observe the prayers.' "

"We asked, 'O Messenger of Allah, how quickly will he walk upon the earth?' He said, 'Like a cloud driven by the wind. He will come to the people and call them (to a false religion), and they will believe in him and respond to him. He will issue a command to the sky, and it will rain; and to the earth, and it will produce crops. After grazing on these crops, their animals will return with their udders full of milk and their flanks stretched. Then he will come to another people and will call them (to a false religion), but they will reject his call. He will depart from them; they will suffer famine and will possess nothing in the form of wealth. Then he will pass through the wasteland and will say, Bring forth your treasures, and the treasures will come forth, like swarms of bees. Then he will call a man brimming with youth; he will strike him with a sword and cut him in two, then place the two pieces at the distance between an archer and his target. Then he will call him, and the young man will come running and laughing.' "

"At that point, Allah will send the Messiah, son of Mary, and he will descend to the white minaret in the east of Damascus, wearing two garments dyed with saffron, placing his hands on the wings of two angels. When he lowers his head, beads of perspiration will fall from it, and when he raises his head, beads like pearls will scatter from it. Every *Kāfir* who smells his fragrance will die, and his breath will reach as far as he can see. He will search for the Dajjāl until he finds him at the gate of Ludd, where he will kill him."

"Then a people whom Allah has protected will come to Jesus son of Mary, and he will wipe their faces [i.e. wipe the traces of hardship from their faces] and tell them of their status in Paradise. At that time Allah will reveal to Jesus: "I have brought forth some of My servants whom no-one will be able to fight. Take My servants safely to *al-Ṭūr*."

"Then Allah will send Gog and Magog, and they will swarm down from every slope. The first of them will pass by the Lake of Tiberias, and will drink some of its water; the last of them will pass by it and say, "There used to be water here." Jesus, the Prophet of Allah, and his Companions will be beseiged until a bull's head will be dearer to them than one hundred dinars are to you nowadays."

"Then Jesus and his Companions will pray to Allah, and He will send insects who will bite the people of Gog and Magog on their necks, so that in the morning they will all perish as one. Then Jesus and his Companions will come down and will not find any nook or cranny on earth which is free from their putrid stench. Jesus and his Companions will again pray to Allah, Who will send birds like the necks of camels; they will seize the bodies of Gog and Magog and throw them wherever Allah wills. Then Allah will send rain which no house or tent will be able to keep out, and the earth will be cleansed, until it will look like a mirror. Then the earth will be told to bring forth its fruit and restore its blessing. On that day, a group of people will be able to eat from a single pomegranate and seek shelter under its skin (i.e. the fruit would be so big). A milch camel will give so much milk that a whole party will be able to drink from it; a cow will give so much milk that a whole tribe will be able to drink from it; and a milch-sheep will give so much milk that a whole family will be able to drink from it. At that time, Allah will send a pleasant wind which will soothe them even under their armpits, and will take the soul of every Muslim. Only the most wicked people will be left, and they will fornicate like asses; then the Last Hour will come upon them.' " (Muslim.)[1]

**FOOTNOTE.**

1. Muslim: *Kitāb al-Fitan wa Ashrāṭ al-Sā'ah*, 8/196-199. Ludd: the biblical Lydda, now known as Lod, site of the zionist state's major airport.

## Chapter 14

# A *ḤADĪTH* NARRATED FROM ABŪ UMĀMAH AL-BĀHILĪ

Abū Umāmah al-Bāhilī said, "The Prophet (S) delivered a speech to us, most of which dealt with the Dājjal and warned us against him. He said, 'No tribulation on earth since the creation of Adam will be worse than the tribulation of the Dajjāl. Allah has never sent a Prophet who did not warn his *Ummah* against the Dajjāl. I am the last of the Prophets, and you are the last *Ummah*. The Dajjāl is emerging among you and it is inevitable. If he appears while I am still among you, I will contend with him on behalf of every Muslim. But if he appears after I am gone, then every person must contend with him on his own behalf, and Allah will take care of every Muslim on my behalf. He will appear on the way between Syria and Iraq, and will spread disaster right and left. O servants of Allah, adhere to the path of Truth. I shall describe him for you in a way that no Prophet has ever done before.

He will start by saying that he is a Prophet, but there will be no Prophet after me. Then he will say, "I am your Lord," but you will never see your Lord until you die. The Dajjāl is one-eyed, but your Lord, glorified be He, is not one-eyed. On his forehead will be written the word *Kāfir*, which every Muslim, literate or illiterate, will be able to read. Among the tribulations he will bring will be the Paradise and Hell he will offer; but that which he calls Hell will be Paradise, and that which he calls Paradise will be Hell. Whoever enters his Hell, let him seek refuge with Allah and recite the opening *Āyāt* of *Sūrat al-Kahf*, and it will become cool and peaceful for him, as the fire became cool and peaceful for Abraham.

"He will say to a Bedouin, What do you think if I bring your father and mother back to life for you? Will you bear witness that I am your lord? The Bedouin will say Yes, so two devils will assume the appearance of his father and mother, and will say, "O my son, follow him for he is your lord."

"He will be given power over one person, whom he will kill and cut in two with a saw. Then he will say, Look at this slave of mine, now I will resurrect him, but he will still claim that he has a Lord other than me. Allah will resurrect him, and this evil man (the Dajjāl) will say to him, Who is your Lord? The man will answer, My Lord is Allah, and you are the enemy of Allah. You are the Dajjāl. By Allah, I have never been more sure of this than I am today."

Abu Sa'īd said, "The Prophet (S) said, 'That man will have the highest status among my *Ummah* in Paradise.' "

Abu Sa'īd said, "By Allah, we never thought that that man would be any other than 'Umar ibn al-Khaṭṭāb, until he passed away."

Al-Muḥāribī said: 'Then we referred to the *Ḥadīth* of Abū Rāfi'ī, which said, "Part of his *Fitnah* will be the fact that he will pass through an area whose people will deny him, and none of their livestock will remain alive. Then he will pass through a second area whose people will believe in him; he will order the sky to rain and the earth to bring forth crops, and their flocks will return from grazing fatter than they have ever been, with their flanks stretched, their udders full. He will pass through every place on earth – except Makkah and Madīnah, which he will never enter, for there are angels guarding every gate of them with unsheathed swords – until he reaches al-Ẓarīb al-Aḥmar and camps at the edge of the salt-marsh. Madīnah will be shaken by three tremors, after which every *Munāfiq* (hypocrite) will leave it, and it will be cleansed of evil, as iron is cleansed of dross. That day will be called *Yawm al-Khalāṣ* (The Day of Purification)." '

Umm Sharīk bint Abī'l-'Akr said , "O Messenger of Allah, where will the Arabs be at that time?" He said, "At that time they will be few; most of them will be in Bayt al-Maqdis (Jerusalem), and their Imām will be a righteous man. Whilst their Imām is going forward to lead the people in praying *Ṣalāt al-Subḥ* (the morning prayer), Jesus son of Mary will descend. The Imām will step back, to let Jesus lead the people in prayer, but Jesus will place his hand between the man's shoulders and say, 'Go forward and lead the prayer, for the *Iqāmah* was made for you.' So the Imām will lead the people in prayer, and afterwards Jesus (AS) will say, 'Open the gate.' The gate will be opened, and behind it will be the Dajjāl and a thousand Jews, each of them bearing a sword and shield. When the Dajjāl sees Jesus, he will begin to dissolve like salt in water, and will run away. Jesus will say, 'You will remain alive until I strike you with my sword.' He will catch up with him at the eastern gate of Ludd and will kill him. The Jews will be deflated with the help of Allah. There will be no place for them to hide; they will not be able to hide behind any stone, wall, animal or tree – except the boxthorn (*al-Gharqarah*) – without it saying, 'O Muslim servant of Allah! here is a Jew, come and kill him!' " The Prophet (S) said, "The time of the Dajjāl will be forty years; one year like half a year, one year like a month, and one month like a week. The rest of his days will pass so quickly that if one of you were at one of the gates of Madīnah, he would not reach the other gate before evening fell."

Someone asked, "O Messenger of Allah, how will we pray in those shorter days?" He said, "Work out the times of prayer in the same way that you do in these longer days, and then pray." The Prophet (S) said, "Jesus son of Mary will be a just administrator and leader of my *Ummah*. He will break the cross, kill the pigs, and abolish the *Jizyah* (tax on non-Muslims). He will not collect the *Ṣadaqah*, so he will not collect sheep and camels. Mutual enmity and hatred will disappear.

Every harmful animal will be made harmless, so that a small boy will be able to put his hand into a snake's mouth without being harmed, a small girl will be able to make a lion run away from her, and a wolf will go among sheep as if he were a sheepdog. The earth will be filled with peace as a container is filled with water. People will be in complete agreement, and only Allah will be worshipped. Wars will cease, and the authority of Quraysh will be taken away. The earth will be like a silver basin, and will produce fruit so abundantly that a group of people will gather to eat a bunch of grapes or one pomegranate and will be satisfied. A bull will be worth so much money, but a horse will be worth only a few dirhams."

Someone asked, "O Messenger of Allah, why will a horse be so cheap?" He said, "Because it will never be ridden in war." He was asked, "Why will the bull be so expensive?" He said, "Because it will plough the earth. For three years before the Dajjāl emerges, the people will suffer severe hunger. In the first year, Allah will order the sky to withhold a third of its rain, and the earth to withhold two-thirds of its fruits. In the third year, He will order the sky to withhold all of its rain, and the earth to withhold all of its fruits, so that nothing green will grow. Every cloven-hoofed creature will die except for whatever Allah wills." Someone asked, "How will the people live at that time?" He said, "By saying *Lā ilāha illā Allāh, Allāhu Akbar, Subḥān Allāh* and *Al-Ḥamdu-li'llāh*. This will be like food for them."[1]

The Prophet (S) said, "The Dajjāl will come forth, and one of the Believers will go towards him. The armed men of the Dajjāl will ask him, 'Where are you going?' He will say, 'I am going to this one who has come forth.' They will say, 'Kill him!' Then some of them will say to the others, 'Hasn't your lord [i.e. the Dajjāl] forbidden you to kill anyone without his permission?' So they will take him to the Dajjāl, and when the Believer sees him, he will say, 'O People, this is the Dajjāl whom the Prophet (S) told us about'. Then the Dajjāl will order them to seize him and wound him in the head; they will inflict blows all over, even in his back and stomach. The Dajjāl will ask him, 'Don't you believe in me?' He will say, 'You are a false Messiah'. The Dajjāl will order that he be sawn in two from the parting of his hair to his legs; then he will walk between the two pieces. They he will say 'Stand!' and the man will stand up. The Dajjāl will say to him, 'Don't you believe in me?' The believer will say, 'It has only increased my understanding that you are the Dajjāl'. Then he will say, 'O people! he will not treat anyone else in such a manner after me'. The Dajjāl will seize him to slaughter him, but the space between his neck and collar-bone will be turned into copper, and the Dajjāl will not be able to do anything to him. He will take the man by his arms and legs and throw him away; the people will believe that he has been thrown into Hell, whereas in fact he will have been thrown into Paradise." The Prophet (S) said, "He will be the greatest of martyrs in the sight of Allah, the Lord of the Worlds." (Muslim.)[2]

**FOOTNOTES.**

1. Ibn Mājah, *Kitāb al-Fitan*, (*Ḥadīth* 4077), 2: 1363.
   "He will break the cross and kill the pigs", i.e. Christianity will be annulled.
   "He will not collect the *Ṣadaqah* (i.e. *Zakāt*) – because there will be so much wealth, and no-one will be in need of *Ṣadaqah*.
2. Muslim, *Kitāb al-Fitan wa Ashrāṭ al-Sā'ah*, 8/199, 200.

Chapter 15

# THE *ḤADĪTH* OF AL-MUGHĪRAH IBN SHU'BAH

Al-Mughīrah ibn Shu'bah said, "No-one asked the Prophet (S) more questions about the Dajjāl than I did. He said, 'You should not worry about him, because he will not be able to harm you.' I said, 'But they say that he will have much food and water!' He said, 'He is too insignificant in the sight of Allah to have all that'." (Muslim.)

Al-Mughīrah ibn Shu'bah said, "No-one asked the Prophet (S) more questions about the Dajjāl than I did." One of the narrators said, "What did you ask him?" Al-Mughīrah said, "I said, 'They say that the Dajjāl will have a mountain of bread and meat, and a river of water'. The Prophet (S) said, 'He is too insignificant in the sight of Allah to have all that'." (Muslim.)

From these *Aḥādīth*, we can see that Allah will test His servants with the Dajjāl and by the miracles which he will be permitted to perform: as we have already mentioned, the Dajjāl will order the sky to rain for those who accept him, and will order the earth to bring forth its fruits so that they and their livestock will eat of it, and their flocks will return fat and with their udders full of milk. Those who reject the Dajjāl and refuse to believe in him will suffer drought and famine; people and livestock will die, and wealth and supplies of food will be depleted. People will follow the Dajjāl like swarms of bees, and he will kill a young man and bring him back to life.

This is not a kind of magic; it will be something real with which Allah will test His servants at the end of time. Many will be led astray, and many will be guided by it. Those who doubt will disbelieve, but those who believe will be strengthened in their faith.

Al-Qāḍī ‘Iyāḍ and others interpreted the phrase “He is too insignificant in the sight of Allah to have all that” as meaning that the Dajjāl is too insignificant to have anything that could lead the true believers astray, because he is obviously evil and corrupt. Even if he brings great terror, the word *Kāfir* will be clearly written between his eyes; one report explains that it will be written “*Kāf, Fā’, Rā’,* ” from which we can understand that it will be written perceptibly, not abstractly, as some people say.

One of his eyes will be blind, protruding and repulsive; this is the meaning of the *Ḥadīth*: “. . . as if it were a grape floating on the surface of the water.” Other reports say that it is “dull, with no light in it,” or “like white spittle on a wall,” i.e., it will look ugly.

Some reports say that it is his right eye which will be blind; others say that it is his left eye.

He could be partly blind in both eyes, or there could be a fault in both eyes. This interpretation could be supported by the *Ḥadīth* narrated by al-Ṭabarānī, in which he reports that Ibn ‘Abbās said, “The Prophet (S) said, ‘The Dajjāl is curly-haired and white-skinned. His head is like the branch of a tree; his left eye is blind, and the other eye looks like a floating grape.’ ”

One may ask: if the Dajjāl is going to cause such widespread evil and his claim to be a “lord” will be so widely believed – even though he is obviously a liar, and all the Prophets have warned against him – why does the Qur’ān not mention him by name and warn us against his lies and stubbornness?

The answer is:-

1. The Dajjāl was referred to in the *Āyah*:
   “. . . The day that certain of the signs of thy Lord do come, no good will it do to a soul to believe in them then, if it believed not before nor earned righteousness through its Faith . . .” (*al-An‘ām* 6:158)

Abū Hurayrah said, "The Prophet (S) said, 'There are three things which, when they appear, no good will it do a soul to believe in them then, if it believed not before nor earned righteousness through its Faith.' They are: The Dajjāl, the Beast, and the rising of the sun from the west.' "

2. Jesus son of Mary will descend from Heaven and kill the Dajjāl, as we have already mentioned. The descent of Jesus is mentioned in the *Āyāt*:

> "That they said (in boast), 'We killed Christ Jesus the son of Mary, the Apostle of God;' – but they killed him not nor crucified him, but so it was made to appear to them, and those who differ therein are full of doubts, with no (certain) knowledge, but only conjecture to follow, for of a surety they killed him not:-
> Nay, God raised him up unto Himself; and God is exalted in Power, Wise; –
> And there is none of the People of the Book but must believe in him before his death; and on the Day of Judgement, he will be a witness against them."
> (*al-Nisā'* 4:157-9)

We think that the *Tafsīr* (interpretation) of this *Āyah* is that the pronoun in "before his death" (*qabla mawtihi*) refers to Jesus; i.e., he will descend and the People of the Book who differed concerning him will believe in him. The Christians claimed that he was divine, while the Jews made a slanderous accusation, i.e. that he was born from adultery. When Jesus descends before the Day of Judgement, he will correct all these differences and lies.

On this basis, the reference to the descent of the Messiah Jesus son of Mary also includes a reference to the Dajjāl (false Messiah or Antichrist), who is the opposite of the true Messiah, because sometimes the Arabs refer to one of two opposites and not the other, but mean both.

3. The Dajjāl is not mentioned by name in the Qur'ān because he is so insignificant: he claims to be divine, but he is merely a human being. His affairs are too contemptible to be mentioned in the Qur'ān. But the Prophets, out of loyalty to Allah, warned their people about the Dajjāl and the tribulations and misguiding miracles he would bring. It is enough for us to know the reports of the Prophets and the many reports from the Prophet Muḥammad (S).

One could argue that Allah has mentioned Pharaoh and his false claims, such as "I am your Lord, Most High" (*al-Nāzi'āt* 79:24) and "O Chiefs! No god do I know for you but myself . . ." (*al-Qaṣaṣ* 28:38), in the Qur'ān. This can be explained by the fact that Pharaoh and his deeds are in the past, and his lies are clear to every believer. But the Dajjāl is yet to come, in the future; it will be a *Fitnah* and a test for all people. So the Dajjāl is not mentioned in the Qur'ān because he is contemptible; and the fact that he is not mentioned means that it will be a greater test.

The facts about the Dajjāl and his lies are obvious and do not need further emphasis. This is often the case when something is very clear. For example, when the Prophet (S) was terminally ill, he wanted to write a document confirming that Abū Bakr would be the *Khalīfah* after him. Then he abandoned this idea, and said, "Allah and the believers will not accept anyone other than Abū Bakr." He decided not to write the document because he knew of Abū Bakr's high standing among the *Ṣaḥābah* (Companions) and was sure that they would not choose anyone else. Similarly, the facts about the Dajjāl are so clear that they did not need to be mentioned in the Qur'ān.

Allah did not mention the Dajjāl in the Qur'ān because He SWT knew that the Dajjāl would not be able to lead His true servants astray; he would only increase their faith, their submission to Allah and His Messenger, their belief in the Truth, and their rejection of falsehood. For this reason the believer whom the

Dajjāl overpowers will say, when he revives him, "By Allah, it has only increased my understanding that you are the one-eyed liar about whom the Prophet (S) spoke".

Chapter 16

# MORE *AḤĀDĪTH* ABOUT THE DAJJĀL

The Prophet (S) said, "The Dajjāl will emerge in a land in the east called Khurāsān. His followers will be people with faces like hammered shields."

Asmā' bint Yazīd al-Anṣāriyyah said, "The Prophet (S) said, 'During the three years just before the Dajjāl comes, there will be one year when the sky will withhold one third of its rain and the earth one-third of its fruits. In the second year the sky will withhold two-thirds of its rain, and the earth two-thirds of its fruits. In the third year the sky will withhold all of its rain, and the earth all of its fruits, and all the animals will die. It will be the greatest tribulation: the Dajjāl will bring a Bedouin and say to him, "What if I bring your camels to life for you? Will you agree that I am your lord?" The Bedouin will say "Yes." So devils will assume the forms of his camels, with the fullest udders and the highest humps. Then he will bring a man whose father and brother have died, and will ask him, "What do you think if I bring your father and brother back to life? Will you agree that I am your lord?" The man will say "Yes," so the devils will assume the forms of his father and brother.' Then the Prophet (S) went out for something, and then returned. The people were very concerned about what he had told them. He stood in the doorway and asked, 'What is wrong, Asmā'?' I said, 'O Messenger of Allah, you have terrified us with what you said about the Dajjāl.' He said, 'He will certainly appear. If I am still alive, I will contend with him on your behalf; otherwise Allah will take care of every Muslim on my behalf.' I said, 'O Messenger of Allah, we do not bake our dough until we are hungry, so how will it be for the believers at that time?' The Prophet (S) said, 'The glorification of Allah which suffices the people of Heaven will be sufficient for them.' "[2]

Abū Hurayrah (RA) said, "The Prophet (S) said, 'The Hour will not come until the Muslims fight the Jews and kill them. When a Jew hides behind a rock or a tree, it will say, "O Muslim, O servant of Allah! There is a Jew behind me, come and kill him!" All the trees will do this except the box-thorn (*al-Gharqad*), because it is the tree of the Jews.' " (Aḥmad.)[3]

**FOOTNOTES.**

1. Tirmidhī, *Abwāb al-Fitan*, *Ḥadīth* 2338, 6/495
   Ibn Mājah, *Kitāb al-Fitan*, *Ḥadīth* 4072, 1354, 2/1353, 1354.
   Aḥmad, *Musnad*, 1/7.
2. Aḥmad, *Musnad*, 6/455, 456.
3. Muslim, *Kitāb al-Fitan wa Ashrāṭ al-Sā'ah*, 8/388.
   Aḥmad, *Musnad*, 2/417.

Chapter 17

# PROTECTION AGAINST THE DAJJĀL

### 1. Seeking refuge with Allah from his tribulation.

It is proven in the *Ṣaḥīḥ* (authentic) *Aḥādīth* that the Prophet (S) used to seek refuge with Allah from the tribulation of the Dajjāl in his prayers, and that he commanded his Ummah to do likewise:

"*Allāhumma innā na'ūdhu bika min 'adhābi jahannam, wa min 'adhābi 'l-qabr, wa min fitnatī 'l-maḥyā'i wa'l-mamāt, wa min fitnati' l-masīḥi 'd-dajjāl.*"

"O Allah! We seek refuge with You from the punishment of Hell, from the punishment of the grave, from the tribulations of life and death, and from the tribulation of the False Messiah (Dajjāl)."[1] This *Ḥadīth* was narrated by many *Ṣaḥābah*, including Anas, Abū Hurayrah, 'Ā'ishah, Ibn 'Abbās, and Sa'd.

### 2. Memorizing certain *Āyāt* from *Sūrat al-Kahf*.

Al-Ḥāfiẓ al-Dhahabī said, "Seeking refuge with Allah from the Dajjāl is mentioned in many *Mutawātir Aḥādīth* (those with numerous lines of narrators). One way of doing this is to memorize ten *Āyāt* from *Sūrat al-Kahf*."

Abū'l-Dirā reported that the Prophet (S) said, "Whoever memorizes the first ten *Āyāt* of *Sūrat al-Kahf* will be protected from the Dajjāl." (Abū Dāwūd.)[2]

### 3. Keeping away from the Dajjāl.

One way to be protected from the tribulation of the Dajjāl is to live in Madīnah or Makkah.

Abū Hurayrah reported that the Prophet (S) said, "There are angels standing at the gates of Madīnah;

neither plague nor the Dajjāl can enter it." (Bukhārī, Muslim.)

Abū Bakr reported that the Prophet (S) said, "The terror caused by the Dajjāl will not enter Madīnah. At that time it will have seven gates; there will be two angels guarding every gate." (Bukhārī.)[3]

Anas said, "The Prophet (S) said, 'The Dajjāl will come to Madīnah, and he will find angels guarding it. Neither plague nor the Dajjāl will enter it, *in shā' Allah*.'" (Tirmidhī, Bukhārī.)

It has been proven in the *Ṣaḥīḥ Aḥādīth* that the Dajjāl will not enter Makkah or Madīnah, because the angels will prevent him from entering these two places which are sanctuaries and are safe from him. When he camps at the salt-marsh (*Sabkhah*) of Madīnah, it will be shaken by three tremors – either physically or metaphorically – and every hypocrite will go out to join the Dajjāl. On that day, Madīnah will be cleansed of its dross and will be refined and purified; and Allah knows best.

**FOOTNOTES.**

1. Bukhārī, *Kitāb al-Janā'iz*, 2/124.
   Muslim, *Kitāb al-Masājid*, 2/93.
2. Muslim, *Kitāb al-Musāfirun*, 2/199.
   Abū Dāwūd, *Kitāb al-Malāḥim* (*Ḥadīth* 4301), 11/401, 402.
3. Bukhārī, *Bāb Ḥaram al-Madīnah*, 1/28.

Chapter 18

# THE LIFE AND DEEDS OF THE DAJJĀL

The Dajjāl will be a man, created by Allah to be a test for people at the end of time. Many will be led astray through him, and many will be guided through him; only the sinful will be led astray.

Al-Ḥāfiẓ Ibn ʻAlī al-Ābār wrote in his book of history (*al-Tārīkh*) that the Dajjāl's *Kunyah* (nickname or paternal title) would be Abū Yūsuf.

Abū Bakrah said, "The Prophet (S) said, 'The Dajjāl's parents will remain childless for thirty years, then a one-eyed child will be born to them. He will be very bad and will cause a great deal of trouble. When he sleeps, his eyes will be closed but his heart (or mind) will still be active.' Then he described his parents: 'His father will be a tall and bulky man, with a long nose like a beak; his mother will be a huge, heavy-breasted woman.' "

Abū Bakrah said, "We heard that a child had been born to some of the Jews in Madīnah. Al-Zubayr ibn al-ʻAwām and I went to see his parents, and found that they matched the description given by the Prophet (S). We saw the boy lying in the sun, covered with a blanket, murmuring to himself. We asked his parents about him, and they said, 'We remained childless for thirty years, then this one-eyed boy was born to us. He is very bad and causes a great deal of trouble.' When we went out, we passed the boy. He asked us, 'What were you doing?' We said, 'Did you hear us?' He said, 'Yes; when I sleep, my eyes are closed but my heart (mind) is still active.' That boy was Ibn Ṣayyād." (Aḥmad, Tirmidhī; this *Ḥadīth* is not very strong.)[1]

As we have already seen in the *Ṣaḥīḥ Aḥādīth*, Mālik and others think that Ibn Ṣayyād was not the Dajjāl;

he was one of a number of "lesser dajjāls". Later he repented and embraced Islam; Allah knows best his heart and deeds.

The "greater" Dajjāl is the one mentioned in the *Ḥadīth* of Fāṭimah bint Qays, which she narrated from the Prophet (S), from Tamīm al-Dārī, and which includes the story of the Jassāsah. The Dajjāl will be permitted to appear at the end of time, after the Muslims have conquered a Roman city called Constantinople. He will first appear in Iṣfahān, in an area known as the Jewish quarter (*al-Yahūdiyyah*). He will be followed by seventy thousand Jews from that area, all of them armed. Seventy thousand Tatars and many people from Khurāsān will also follow him. At first he will appear as a tyrannical king, then he will claim to be a prophet, then a lord. Only the most ignorant of men will follow him; the righteous and those guided by Allah will reject him. He will start to conquer the world country by country, fortress by fortress, region by region, town by town; no place will remain unscathed except Makkah and Madīnah. The length of his stay on earth will be forty days: one day like a year, one day like a month, one day like a week, and the rest of the days like normal days, i.e. his stay will be approximately one year and two and a half months. Allah will grant him many miracles, through which whoever He wills will be led astray, and the faith of the believers will be strengthened. The descent of Jesus son of Mary, the true Messiah, will happen at the time of the Dajjāl, the false messiah. He will descend to the minaret in the east of Damascus. The believers and true servants of Allah will gather to support him, and the Messiah Jesus son of Mary will lead them against the Dajjāl, who at that time will be heading for Bayt al-Maqdis (Jerusalem). He will catch up with him at 'Aqabah 'Afīq. The Dajjāl will run away from him, but Jesus will catch up with him at the gate of Ludd, and will kill him with his spear just as he is entering it. He will say to him, "I have to deal you a blow; you cannot escape."

When the Dajjāl faces him, he will begin to dissolve like salt in water. So Jesus will kill him with his spear at the gate of Ludd, and he will die there, as many *Ṣaḥīḥ Aḥādīth* indicate.

Majma' ibn Jāriyah is reported to have said, "I heard the Prophet (S) saying, 'The son of Mary will kill the Dajjāl at the gate of Ludd.'" (Tirmidhī.)[2]

**FOOTNOTES.**

1. Tirmidhī, *Abwāb al-Fitan* (*Ḥadīth* 2350), 6/522, 523. Aḥmad, *Musnad*, 5/40.
   "When he sleeps, his eyes will be closed but his heart (or mind) will still be active" – meaning that, his evil ideas will still come to him even while he is asleep.
2. Tirmidhī, *Abwāb al-Fitan* (*Ḥadīth* 2345), 6/513, 514.

## Chapter 19

# THE DESCENT OF JESUS AT THE END OF TIME

'Abd Allāh ibn 'Amr said, "The Prophet (S) said, 'The Dajjāl will appear in my *Ummah*, and will remain for forty – "I cannot say whether he meant forty days, forty months or forty years." – Then Allah will send Jesus son of Mary, who will resemble 'Urwah ibn Mas'ūd. He will chase the Dajjāl and kill him. Then the people will live for seven years during which there will be no enmity between any two persons. Then Allah will send a cold wind from the direction of Syria, which will take the soul of everyone who has the slightest speck of good or faith in his heart. Even if one of you were to enter the heart of a mountain, the wind would reach him there and take his soul. Only the most wicked people will be left; they will be as careless as birds, with the characteristics of beasts, and will have no concern for right and wrong. Satan will come to them in the form of man and will say, "Don't you respond?" They will say, "What do you order us to do?" He will order them to worship idols, and in spite of that they will have sustenance in abundance, and lead comfortable lives.

"Then the Trumpet will be blown, and everyone will tilt their heads to hear it. The first one to hear it will be a man busy repairing a trough for his camels. He and everyone else will be struck down. Then Allah will send (or send down) rain like dew, and the bodies of the people (i.e. the dead) will grow out of it. Then the trumpet will be sounded again, and the people will get up and look around. Then it will be said, "O people, go to your Lord and account for yourselves." It will be said, "Bring out the people of Hell," and it will be asked, "How many are there?" – the answer will come:

"Nine hundred and ninety-nine out of every thousand." On that day a child will grow old and the shin will be laid bare." (*al-Qalam* 68:42) (Muslim.)[1]

Abū Hurayrah said, "The Prophet (S) said, 'The son of Mary will come down as a just leader. He will break the cross, and kill the pigs. Peace will prevail and people will use their swords as sickles. Every harmful beast will be made harmless; the sky will send down rain in abundance, and the earth will bring forth its blessings. A child will play with a fox and not come to any harm; a wolf will graze with sheep and a lion with cattle, without harming them.' " (Aḥmad.)[2]

Abū Hurayrah said, "The Prophet (S) said, 'By Him in Whose hand is my soul, surely the son of Mary will come down among you as a just ruler. He will break the cross, kill the pigs and abolish the *Jizyah*. Wealth will be in such abundance that no-one will care about it, and a single prostration in prayer will be better than the world and all that is in it.' " Abū Hurayrah said, 'If you wish, recite the *Āyah*:

"And there is none of the People of the Book but must believe in him before his death; and on the Day of Judgement he will be a witness against them . . ." (*al-Nisā'* 4:159) (Bukhārī, Muslim.)[3]

Abū Hurayrah reported that the Prophet (S) said, "The Prophets are like brothers; they have different mothers but their religion is one. I am the closest of all the people to Jesus son of Mary, because there is no other Prophet between him and myself. He will come again, and when you see him, you will recognize him. He is of medium height and his colouring is reddish-white. He will be wearing two garments, and his hair will look wet. He will break the cross, kill the pigs, abolish the *Jizyah* and call the people to Islam. During his time, Allah will end every religion and sect other than Islam, and will destroy the Dajjāl. Then peace and security will prevail on earth, so that lions will graze with camels, tigers with cattle, and wolves with sheep; children will be able to play with snakes without coming to any harm. Jesus will remain for forty years, then die, and the Muslims will pray for him." (Aḥmad.)[4]

Ibn Mas'ūd reported that the Prophet (S) said, "On the night of the *Isrā'* (night journey), I met my father Abraham, Moses and Jesus, and they discussed the Hour. The matter was referred first to Abraham, then to Moses, and both said, 'I have no knowledge of it'. Then it was referred to Jesus, who said, 'No-one knows about its timing except Allah; what my Lord told me was that the Dajjāl will appear, and when he sees me he will begin to melt like lead. Allah will destroy him when he sees me. The Muslims will fight against the *Kāfirs*, and even the trees and rocks will say, "O Muslim, there is a *Kāfir* hiding beneath me – come and kill him!" Allah will destroy the *Kāfirs*, and the people will return to their own lands. Then Gog and Magog will appear from all directions, eating and drinking everything they find. The people will complain to me, so I will pray to Allah and He will destroy them, so that the earth will be filled with their stench. Allah will send rain which will wash their bodies into the sea. My Lord has told me that when that happens, the Hour will be very close, like a pregnant woman whose time is due, but her family do not know exactly when she will deliver.' " (Aḥmad, Ibn Mājah.)[5]

**FOOTNOTES.**

1. Muslim, *Kitāb al-Fitan wa Ashrāṭ al-Sā'ah*, 8/201, 202.
2. Aḥmad, *Musnad*, 2/482, 483.
3. Bukhārī, *Kitāb al-Anbiyā'*, 204, 205.
   Muslim, *Kitāb al-Īmān*, 1/93, 94.
4. Aḥmad, *Musnad*, 2/406.
5. Aḥmad, *Musnad*, 1/375.
   Similar *Ḥadīth* in Ibn Mājah, *Kitāb al-Fitan* (*Ḥadīth* 4081), 2/1365, 1366.

Chapter 20

# DESCRIPTION OF THE MESSIAH JESUS SON OF MARY, MESSENGER OF ALLAH

Abū Hurayrah said, "The Prophet (S) said, 'On the night of the *Isrā'* (miraculous journey to Jerusalem) I met Moses – he was a slim man with wavy hair, and looked like a man from the Shanū'ah tribe. I also met Jesus – he was of medium height and of a red complexion, as if he had just come out of the bath.' " (Bukhārī, Muslim.)[1]

The Prophet (S) said, "Whilst I was asleep, I saw myself (in a dream) making *Ṭawāf* around the Ka'bah. I saw a brown-skinned man, with straight hair, being supported by two men, and with water dripping from his head. I said, 'Who is this?' They said, 'The son of Mary.' I turned around and saw a fat, ruddy man, with curly hair, who was blind in his right eye; his eye looked like a floating grape. I asked, 'Who is this?' They said, 'The Dajjāl.' The one who most resembles him is Ibn Qaṭan." Al-Zuhrī explained: Ibn Qaṭan was a man from Khuzā'ah who died during the *Jāhiliyyah* (before the coming of Islam). (Bukhārī.)[2]

**FOOTNOTES.**

1. Bukhārī, *Kitāb al-Anbiyā'*, 4/302.
   Muslim, *Kitāb al-Īmān*, 1/106, 107.
2. Bukhārī, *ibid.*

Chapter 21

# THE APPEARANCE OF GOG AND MAGOG

They (two tribes or peoples) will appear at the time of Jesus son of Mary, after the Dajjāl. Allah will destroy them all in one night, in response to the supplication of Jesus.

Abū Hurayrah reported that the Prophet (S) said, "Every day, Gog and Magog are trying to dig a way out through the barrier. When they begin to see sunlight through it, the one who is in charge of them says, 'Go back; you can carry on digging tomorrow,' and when they come back, the barrier is stronger than it was before. This will continue until their time comes and Allah wishes to send them forth. They will dig until they begin to see sunlight, then the one who is in charge of them will say, 'Go back; you can carry on digging tomorrow, *in shā'Allah*.' In this case he will make an exception by saying *in shā'Allah*, thus relating the matter to the Will of Allah. They will return on the following day, and find the hole as they left it. They will carry on digging and come out against the people. They will drink all the water, and the people will entrench themselves in their fortresses. Gog and Magog will fire their arrows into the sky, and they will fall back to earth with something like blood on them. Gog and Magog will say, 'We have defeated the people of earth, and overcome the people of heaven.' Then Allah will send a kind of worm in the napes of their necks, and they will be killed by it . . . 'By Him in Whose hand is the soul of Muḥammad, the beasts of the earth will become fat.' "[1]

Gog and Magog are two groups of Turks, descended from Yāfith (Japheth), the father of the Turks, one of the sons of Noah. At the time of Abraham (AS), there was a king called Dhū'l-Qarnayn. He performed *Ṭawāf* around the Ka'bah with Abraham (AS) when he first built it; he believed and followed him. Dhū'l-Qarnayn was a good man and a great king; Allah gave him great power and he ruled the east and west. He held sway over all kings and countries, and travelled far and wide in both east and west. He travelled eastwards until he reached a pass between two mountains, through which people were coming out. They did not understand anything, because they were so isolated; they were Gog and Magog. They were spreading corruption through the earth, and harming the people, so the people sought help from Dhū'l-Qarnayn. They asked him to build a barrier between them and Gog and Magog. He asked them to help him to build it, so together they built a barrier by mixing iron, copper and tar.

Thus Dhū'l-Qarnayn restrained Gog and Magog behind the barrier. They tried to penetrate the barrier, or to climb over it, but to no avail. They could not succeed because the barrier is so huge and smooth. They began to dig, and they have been digging for centuries; they will continue to do so until the time when Allah decrees that they come out. At that time the barrier will collapse, and Gog and Magog will rush out in all directions, spreading corruption, uprooting plants, killing people. When Jesus (AS) prays against them, Allah will send a kind of worm in the napes of their necks, and they will be killed by it.

**FOOTNOTES.**

1. Tirmidhī, *Abwāb al-Tafsīr: Sūrat al-Kahf* (*Ḥadīth* 5160), 8/597-99)
   Ibn Mājah, *Kitāb al-Fitan*, (*Ḥadīth* 4080), 2/1364.
   Aḥmad, *Musnad*, 2/510, 511.

## Chapter 22

# THE DESTRUCTION OF THE KA'BAH

At the end of time, Dhū'l-Suwayqatayn, who will come from Abyssinia (*al-Ḥabash*), will destroy the Ka'bah in order to steal its treasure and *Kiswah* (cloth covering). The Ka'bah is the ancient building which was built by Abraham, and whose foundations were laid by Adam.

As *Tafsīr* (interpretation) of the *Āyah* "Until the Gog and Magog (people) are let through (their barrier) . . ." (*al-Anbiyā'* 21:96), it was reported from Ka'b al-Aḥbar that Dhū'l-Suwayqatayn will first emerge at the time of Jesus, son of Mary. Allah will send Jesus at the head of a vanguard of between seven and eight hundred. While they are marching towards Dhū'l-Suwayqatayn, Allah will send a breeze from the direction of Yemen, which will take the soul of every believer. Only the worst of people will be left, and they will begin to copulate like animals. Ka'b said: "At that time, the Hour will be close at hand."[1]

'Abd Allah ibn 'Amr said, "I heard the Prophet (S) say, 'Dhū'l-Suwayqatayn from Abyssinia will destroy the Ka'bah and steal its treasure and *Kiswah*. It is as if I could see him now: he is bald-headed and has a distortion in his wrists. He will strike the Ka'bah with his spade and pick-axe'." (Aḥmad.)[2]

It was reported from 'Abd Allāh ibn 'Umar that the Prophet (S) said, "Leave the Abyssinians alone so long as they do not disturb you, for no-one will recover the treasure of the Ka'bah except Dhū'l-Suwayqatayn from Abyssinia." (Abū Dāwūd, in the chapter on the prohibition of provoking the Abyssinians.)[3]

Ibn 'Abbās narrated that the Prophet (S) said, "It is

as if I can see him now: he is black and his legs are widely spaced. He will destroy the Ka'bah stone by stone." (Aḥmad.)[4]

The Prophet (S) said, "The Hour will not come until a man from Qaḥṭān appears and rules the people." (Muslim; similar *Ḥadīth* in Bukhārī.) This man could be Dhū'l-Suwayqatayn, or someone else, because this man comes from Qaḥṭān, while other reports say that Dhū'l-Suwayqatayn comes from Abyssinia; and Allah knows best.

Abū Hurayrah said, "The Prophet (S) said, 'Day and night will not come to an end until a freedman called Jahjāh holds sway.'" (Aḥmad.) This could be the name of Dhū'l-Suwayqatayn from Abyssinia; and Allah knows best.

'Umar ibn al-Khaṭṭāb reported that he heard the Prophet (S) say: "The people of Makkah will leave, and only a few people will pass through it. Then it will be resettled and rebuilt; then the people will leave it again, and no-one will ever return."[5]

**FOOTNOTES.**

1. Concerning Dhū'l-Suwayqatayn, see: Bukhārī: *Kitāb al-Ḥajj*, *Bāb Hadam al-Ka'bah* (The Book of Pilgrimage, Chapter of the Destruction of the Ka'bah), 2/183.
   Muslim, *Kitāb al-Fatan wa Ashrāṭ al-Sā'ah*, 8/183.
   Dhū'l-Suwayqatayn: *al-Suwayqatayn* is the diminutive of *al-Sāqayn* (legs); his legs are described as being "small" because they are thin. Thin legs are, in general, a characteristic of the Sudanese and people of the Horn of Africa.
2. Aḥmad, *Musnad*, 2/220.
3. Abū Dāwūd, *Kitāb al-Malāḥim*, (*Ḥadīth* 4287), 11/423.
4. Aḥmad, *Musnad*, 1/227.
5. *op. cit.*, 1/23.

## Chapter 23

# MADĪNAH WILL REMAIN INHABITED AT THE TIME OF THE DAJJĀL

It has been proven in the *Ṣaḥīḥ Aḥādīth*, as already stated, that the Dajjāl will not be able to enter Makkah and Madīnah, and that there will be angels at the gates of Makkah to ward him off and prevent him from entering.

It was reported from Abū Hurayrah that the Prophet (S) said, "Neither the Dajjāl nor plague will be able to enter Madīnah." As mentioned above, the Dajjāl will camp outside Madīnah, and it will be shaken by three tremors. Every hypocrite and sinner will go out to join the Dajjāl, and every believer and Muslim will stay. That day will be called the Day of Purification (*Yawm al-Khalāṣ*). Most of those who go out to join the Dajjāl will be women. As the Prophet (S) said, "Verily it (Madīnah) is good; its evil will be eliminated and its goodness will be obvious."

Allah SWT said:

"Women impure are for men impure, and men impure for women impure, and women of purity are for men of purity, and men of purity are for women of purity . . ." (*al-Nūr* 24:26)

Madīnah will remain inhabited during the days of the Dajjāl, and during the time of Jesus son of Mary (AS), until he dies and is buried there. Then it will be destroyed.

'Umar ibn al-Khaṭṭāb said, "I heard the Prophet (S) say, 'A rider will go around Madīnah and say, There used to be many Muslims here.'" (Aḥmad.)[1]

**FOOTNOTES.**

1. Aḥmad, *Musnad*, 1/20.

## Chapter 24

# THE EMERGENCE OF THE BEAST

Among the signs of the Hour will be the emergence of a beast from the earth. It will be very strange in appearance, and extremely huge; one cannot even imagine what it will look like. It will emerge from the earth and shake the dust from its head. It will have with it the ring of Solomon and the rod of Moses. People will be terrified of it and will try to run away, but they will not be able to escape, because such will be the decree of Allah. It will destroy the nose of every unbeliever with the rod, and write the word "*Kāfir*" on his forehead; it will adorn the face of every believer and write the word "*Mu'min*" (true believer) on his forehead, and it will speak to people.

Allah SWT said:

"And when the Word is fulfilled against them (the unjust), We shall produce from the earth a Beast to (face) them: it will speak to them, . . ."
(*al-Naml* 27·82)

Ibn 'Abbās, al-Ḥasan and Qutādah said that "It will speak to them" (*tukallimuhum*) means that it will address them. Ibn Jarīr suggested that it means that the Beast will address them with the words ". . . for that mankind did not believe with assurance in Our Signs" (*al-Naml* 27:82 – latter part of the *Āyah*). Ibn Jarīr reported this from 'Alī and 'Aṭā'. It was reported from Ibn 'Abbās that *tukallimuhum* means that the Beast will cut them, i.e., it will write the word "*Kāfir*" on the forehead of the unbeliever and "*Mu'min*" on the forehead of the believer. It was also reported from Ibn 'Abbās that he will both address them and cut them; this suggestion incorporates both of the previous suggestions; and Allah knows best.

We have already mentioned the *Ḥadīth* of Ḥudhayfah ibn Usayd, in which the Prophet (S) is reported to have said, "The Hour will not come until you see ten signs: the smoke; the Dajjāl; the Beast; the sun rising from the West; the descent of Jesus son of Mary; Gog and Magog; and three land-slides – one in the East, one in the West, and one in Arabia, at the end of which fire will burst forth from the direction of Aden (Yemen) and drive people to the place of their final assembly."

Abū Hurayrah said: "The Prophet (S) said, 'Hasten to do good deeds before six things happen: the rising of the sun from the West, the smoke, the Dajjāl, the Beast, the (death) of one of you or general tribulation." (Muslim.)

Barīdah said: "The Prophet (S) took me to a place in the desert, near Makkah. It was a dry piece of land surrounded by sand. The Prophet (S) said, 'The Beast will emerge from this place.' It was a very small area." (Ibn Mājah.)[1]

It was reported from Abū Hurayrah that the Prophet (S) said, "The Beast of the Earth will emerge, and will have with it the rod of Moses and the ring of Solomon." It was also reported that he said, "(The Beast) will destroy the noses of the unbelievers with the ring, – so that people seated around one table will begin to address one another with the words "O Believer!" or "O Unbeliever!" (i.e., everyone's status will become clear). (Ibn Mājah.)[2]

'Abd Allāh ibn 'Amr said, "I memorized a *Ḥadīth* from the Prophet (S) which I have not forgotten since. I heard the Prophet (S) say, 'The first of the signs (of the Hour) to appear will be the rising of the sun from the West and the appearance of the Beast before the people in the forenoon. Whichever of these two events happens first, the other will follow immediately.'" (Muslim.)[3] That is to say, these will be the first extraordinary signs. The Dajjāl, the descent of Jesus (AS), the emergence of Gog and Magog, are less unusual in that they are all human beings. But the emergence of the Beast, whose form will be very strange, its addressing the people and classifying them according to their faith or unbelief, is something truly extraordinary. This is the first of the earthly signs, as the rising of the sun from the West is the first of the heavenly signs.

**FOOTNOTES.**

1. Ibn Mājah, *Kitāb al-Fitan*, (*Ḥadīth* 4267), 2/1352.
2. Similar *Ḥadīth* narrated by Ibn Mājah in *Kitāb al-Fitan* (*Ḥadīth* 4061), 2 – 1351, 1352.
   Aḥmad, *Musnad*, 2 – 295.
3. Muslim, *Kitāb al-Fitan*, 8/202.

## Chapter 25

# THE RISING OF THE SUN FROM THE WEST

Allah SWT says:

"Are they waiting to see if the angels come to them, or thy Lord (Himself), or certain of the Signs of thy Lord? The day that certain of the signs of thy Lord do come, no good will it do to a soul to believe in them then, if it believed not before nor earned righteousness through its faith. Say: 'Wait ye: we too are waiting'." (*al-An'ām* 6:158.)

It was reported from Abu Sa'īd al-Khudrī that the Prophet (S) explained, "The day that certain of the Signs of thy Lord do come, no good will it do to a soul to believe in them then", referring to the rising of the sun from the West. (Aḥmad.)[1]

Abū Hurayrah said, "The Prophet (S) said, 'The Hour will not come until the sun rises from the West. When the people see it, whoever is living on earth will believe, but that will be the time when – No good will it do to a soul to believe in them then, if it believed not before.'" (Bukhārī.)[2]

It was also reported from Abū Hurayrah that the Prophet (S) said, "The Hour will not come until the sun rises from the West. When it rises and the people see it, they will all believe. But that will be the time when 'No good will it do to a soul to believe in them then'." (Bukhārī.)[3]

It was reported from Abū Hurayrah that the Prophet (S) said, "There are three things which, if they appear, 'No good will it do to a soul to believe in them then, if it believed not before nor earned righteousness through its faith'. They are: the rising of the sun from the West, the Dajjāl, and the Beast of the Earth." (Aḥmad,

Muslim, Tirmidhī.)[4]

Abū Dharr said, "The Prophet (S) asked me, 'Do you know where the sun goes when it sets?' I said, 'I do not know.' He said, 'It travels until it prostrates itself beneath the Throne, and asks for permission to rise again. But a time will come when it will be told, 'Go back whence you came.' That will be the time when 'No good will it do to a soul to believe in them then, if it believed not before nor earned righteousness through its faith'." (Bukhārī.)[5]

'Amr ibn Jarīr said, "Three Muslims were sitting with Marwān in Madīnah, and heard him say, whilst talking about the Signs of the Hour, that the first of them would be the appearance of the Dajjāl. The three went to 'Abd Allāh ibn 'Amr, and told him what they had heard Marwān say concerning the Signs. 'Abd Allāh said, 'Marwān has not said much. I memorized a *Ḥadīth* like that from the Prophet (S) which I have not forgotten since. I heard the Prophet (S) say: The first of the signs will be the rising of the sun from the West, and the emergence of the Beast in the forenoon. Whichever of the two comes first, the other will follow immediately.' "

"Then 'Abd Allāh, who was widely-read, said, 'I think that the first to happen will be the rising of the sun from the West. Every time it sets, it goes beneath the Throne, prostrates itself, and seeks permission to rise again. A time will come when three times it will seek permission and will receive no reply, until, when part of the night has passed and it realizes that even if it were given permission, it would not be able to rise on time, it will say: 'O my Lord, how far the rising-point is from me! What can I do for the people now?' Then it will seek permission to go back, and it will be told: 'Rise from where you are now' – and it will rise from the West'." Then 'Abd Allāh receited the *Āyah*:

"No good will it do to a soul to believe in them then, if it believed not before nor earned righteousness through its faith." (Aḥmad.)[6]

Some scholars interpret "the rising of the sun from

the West" as meaning that Islam will appear in the West, as strong as it was in the beginning, and that the people of the West will carry the flag of Islam.

**FOOTNOTES.**

1. Aḥmad, *Musnad*, 3/31.
2. Bukhārī, *Kitāb al-Tafsīr*, 6/73.
3. Bukhārī, *ibid.*
4. Muslim, *Kitāb al-Īmān*, 1/96.
   Tirmidhī, *Abwāb al-Tafsīr (Ḥadīth* 5067), 8/449, 450.
   Aḥmad, *Musnad*, 2/455, 446.
5. Similar *Ḥadīth* in Bukhārī, *Kitāb Bid' al-Khalq*, 4/131.
6. Aḥmad, *Musnad*, 2/201.

Chapter 26

# THE SMOKE WHICH WILL APPEAR AT THE END OF TIME

Masrūq said: "While a man was giving a speech among the people of Kindah, he said, 'There will be smoke on the Day of Resurrection which will deprive the hypocrites of their hearing and sight, but the believers will only suffer something like a cold'. We were terrified, so we went to Ibn Mas'ūd, who was reclining. When he heard about this, he became angry and sat up, and said: 'O people, whoever knows a thing, let him say it; but whoever does not know, let him say, "Allah knows best." It is a part of knowledge, when one does not know something, to say "Allah knows best." Allah SWT said to His Prophet Muhammad (S): "Say: 'No reward do I ask of you for this (Qur'ān), nor am I a pretender'." (*Ṣād* 38:86.)

"Quraysh were being slow in embracing Islam, so the Prophet (S) prayed against them, saying, 'O *Allah*, help me against them by sending seven years of famine like those of Joseph.' They were afflicted by a year of famine in which they were destroyed, and ate dead animals and bones. They began to see something like smoke between the sky and the earth. Abū Sufyān came and said, 'O Muḥammad! You came to command us to keep good relations with our relatives, and your people have perished, so pray that Allah may relieve them'."

Then Ibn Mas'ūd recited,

"Then watch thou for the Day that the sky will bring forth a kind of smoke (or mist) plainly visible,

Enveloping the people: this will be a Penalty Grievous.

(They will say:) 'Our Lord! Remove the Penalty from us, for we do truly believe!'

How shall the Message be (effectual) for them, seeing

that an Apostle explaining things clearly has (already) come to them?

Yet they return away from him and say: 'Tutored (by others), a man possessed!'

We shall indeed remove the Penalty for a while, (but) truly ye will revert (to your ways)."

(*al-Dukhān* 44:10-15)

Ibn Mas'ūd asked: "Will their punishment in the Hereafter be removed so they can go back to their *Kufr*?"

Allah SWT said:

"One day We shall seize you with a mighty onslaught: We will indeed (then) exact Retribution!"

(*al-Dukhān* 44:16)

". . . and soon will come the inevitable (punishment)!"

(*al-Furqān* 25:77)

These *Āyāt* refer to the Day (Battle) of Badr.

Allah SWT said:

"*Alif – Lām – Mīm*. The Romans (Byzantines) have been defeated – in a land close by; but they, (even) after (this) defeat of theirs, will soon be victorious – within a few years . . ."

(*al-Rūm* 30: 1-3) (Bukhārī.)[1]

This speaker's suggestion – that the idea that the smoke would be on the Day of Resurrection was not a good one – made Ibn Mas'ūd react angrily. But the smoke will appear before the Day of Resurrection; it will be one of the signs, which are: the Beast, the Dajjāl, the Smoke, and Gog and Magog, as the *Aḥādīth* narrated from Abū Ṣarīḥah, Abū Hurayrah and other *Ṣaḥābah* indicate.

As mentioned in the *Ṣaḥīḥ Aḥādīth*, the fire which will appear before the Day of Resurrection will burst forth from the direction of Aden, and drive the people to the place of their final assembly. It will move with them and halt with them, and will devour any who lag behind.

**FOOTNOTES.**

1. Bukhārī, *Kitāb al-Tafsīr – Sūrat al-Rūm*, 6/142, 143.

## Chapter 27

# OTHER EVENTS WHICH WILL PRECEDE THE HOUR

It was reported from Abū Sa'īd al-Khudrī that the Prophet (S) said, "Thunderbolts will increase so much as the Hour approaches that when a man comes to a people, he will ask, 'Who amongst you was struck by a thunderbolt this morning?' and they will say, 'So-and-so and so-and-so was struck'." (Aḥmad.)[1]

**Heavy rain before the Day of Resurrection.**

It was reported from Abū Hurayrah that the Prophet (S) said, "The hour will not come until there has been rain which will destroy all dwellings except tents".[2]

We have already mentioned many *Aḥādīth* about the signs of the Hour. Now we will turn our attention to some *Aḥādīth* which could indicate that the Hour is close at hand.

It was reported from Abū Hurayrah that the Prophet (S) said: "The Hour will not come until the following events have come to pass: people will compete with one another in constructing high buildings; two big groups will fight one another, and there will be many casualties – they will both be following the same religious teaching; earthquakes will increase; time will pass quickly; afflictions and killing will increase; nearly thirty dajjāls will appear, each of them claiming to be a messenger from Allah; a man will pass by a grave and say, 'Would that I were in your place'; the sun will rise from the West; when it rises and the people see it, they will all believe, but that will be the time when 'No good will it do to a soul to believe in them then, if it believed not before' (*al-An'ām* 6:158); and a wealthy man will worry lest no-one accept his *Zakāt*." (Bukhārī, Muslim.)

It was reported from Anas that the Prophet (S) said: "Among the signs of the Hour are the following: knowledge will decrease and ignorance will prevail; fornication and the drinking of wine will be common; the number of men will decrease and the number of women will increase, until one man will look after fifty women." (Bukhārī.)[3]

'Ā'ishah said, "I heard the Prophet (S) say, 'Day and night will not pass away until people begin to worship Lāt and 'Uzzā' (two goddesses of pre-Islamic Arabia). I said, 'O Messenger of Allah, I thought that when Allah revealed the *Āyah* "It is He Who has sent His Apostle with Guidance and the Religion of Truth, to proclaim over all religion, even though the Pagans may detest (it)" (*al-Tawbah* 9:33), it implied that (this promise) would be fulfilled'. The Prophet (S) said, 'It will happen as Allah wishes. Then Allah will send a pleasant breeze, which will take everyone who has as much faith as a grain of mustard-seed in his heart. Only those with no goodness in them will be left, and they will revert to the religion of their forefathers'." (Muslim.)[4]

It was reported from Abū Hurayrah that one day, while the Prophet (S) was sitting with the people, a Bedouin came to him and asked him about *Īmān* and *Islām* . . . then he asked, "O Messenger of Allah, when will the Hour be?" He said, "The one who is asked about it does not know more than the one who asks, but I will tell you about its signs. When a slave gives birth to her mistress, and when the bare-footed and naked become the chiefs of the people – these are among the signs of the Hour. There are five things which no-one knows except Allah." Then he recited:

"Verily the knowledge of the Hour is with God (alone). It is He Who sends down rain, and He Who knows what is in the wombs. Nor does anyone know what it is that he will earn on the morrow: nor does anyone know in what land he is to die. Verily God is All-Knowing, All Aware." (*Luqmān* 31:34.)

Then the man went away, and the Prophet (S) said, "Call him back to me", but when the people went to call him, they could not see anything. The Prophet (S) said, "That was Gabriel, who came to teach the people their religion". (Bukhārī, Muslim.)[5]

"The bare-footed and naked paupers will compete with one another in constructing high buildings" means that they will become the chiefs of people. They will become rich, and their only concern will be to compete in constructing high buildings. This is as in the *Ḥadīth* we shall see later: "The Hour will not come until the happiest people in the world will be the depraved sons of the depraved".

It was reported from Abū Sa'īd that the Prophet (S) said: "The Hour will not come until the time when a man will leave his home, and his shoes or whip or stick will tell what is happening to his family". (Aḥmad.)[6]

It was reported from Abū Sa'īd that the Prophet (S) said: "By Him in Whose hand is my soul, the Hour will not come until wild animals talk to men, and a man speaks to his whip or his shoe, and his thigh will tell him about what happened to his family after he left".[7]

Anas said, "We were discussing the fact that the Hour would not come until there is no rain, the earth does not produce crops, and fifty women will be cared for by one man; and if a woman passes by a man, he will look at her and say, 'This woman once had a husband'." (Aḥmad.)[8]

Abū Hurayrah said: "The Prophet (S) said: 'The Hour will not come until time passes so quickly that a year will be like a month, a month like a week, a week like a day, a day like an hour, and an hour like the time it takes for a palm-leaf to burn'." (Aḥmad.)[9]

Abū Hurayrah said: "The Prophet (S) said: 'The Hour will not come until time passes so quickly that a year will be like a month, a month like a week, a week like a day, a day like an hour, and an hour like the time it takes for a palm-leaf to burn'." (Aḥmad.)[9]

Abū Hurayrah said, "The Prophet (S) said: 'The world will not pass away until the one who enjoys it the most is the depraved son of the depraved'." (Aḥmad.)[10]

Abū Hurayrah said, "The Prophet (S) said, 'Before the Hour comes, there will be years of deceit, in which a truthful person will be disbelieved and a liar will be believed; and the insignificant will have a say'." (Aḥmad.)[11]

Abū Hurayrah said: "I heard the Prophet (S) say: 'The Hour will not come until the sheep with horns no longer fights the sheep without horns'." (Aḥmad.)[12]

It was reported from Abū Hurayrah that the Prophet (S) said, "The Hour will not come until wealth increases so much that a wealthy man will be worried lest no-one accept his *Ṣadaqah*; knowledge will be taken away; time will pass quickly; tribulations will appear; and there will be much *Harj*". The people asked, "What is *Harj*", O Messenger of Allah?" He said, "Killing, killing". (Aḥmad.)[13]

It was reported from Abū Hurayrah that the Prophet (S) said, "By Him Who sent me with the Truth, this earth will not pass away until people are afflicted with landslides, are pelted with stones, and are transformed into animals." The people asked, "When will that be, O Messenger of Allah?" He said, "When you see women riding in the saddle, when singers are common, when bearing false witness becomes widespread, and when men lie with men and women with women".[14]

Ṭāriq ibn Shihāb said, "We were sitting with 'Abd Allah ibn Mas'ūd, when a man came and told us that the time for prayer had come. So we got up and went to the mosque . . . After the prayer, a man came to 'Abd Allāh ibn Mas'ūd and said, *'As-salām 'alayka* (Peace be upon you), O Abū 'Abd al-Raḥmān'. 'Abd Allāh answered, 'Allah and His Messenger have spoken the truth'. When we went back, we asked one another, 'Did you hear the answer he gave? Who is going to ask him about it?' I said, 'I will ask him'; so I asked him when he came out. He narrated from the Prophet (S): 'Before the Hour comes, there will be a special greeting for the people of distinction; trade will become so widespread that a woman will help her husband in business; family ties will be cut; the giving of false witness will be common, while truthful witness will be rare; and writing will be widespread". (Aḥmad.)[15]

**FOOTNOTES.**

1. Aḥmad, *Musnad*, 3/64, 65.
2. Aḥmd, 2/262.
3. Bukhārī, *Kitāb al-'Ilm*, 1/30, 31.
4. Muslim, *Kitāb al-Fitan*, 8/182.
5. Bukhārī, *Kitāb al-Īmān*, 1/19; *Kitāb al-Tafsīr – Sūrat Luqmān*, 6/144.
   Muslim, *Kitāb al-Īmān*, 1/30, 31.
6. Aḥmad, *Musnad*, 3/88, 89.
7. Aḥmad, *Musnad*, 3/83, 84.
8. *op. cit.*, 3/286.
9. *op. cit.*, 3/358.
10. *op. cit.*, 2/358.
11. *op. cit.*, 2/238.
12. *op. cit.*, 2/442.
13. *op. cit.*, 2/313.
14. al-Haythamī, *Kitāb al-Fitan*.
15. Aḥmad, *Musnad*, 1/407.

## Chapter 28

# DESCRIPTION OF THE PEOPLE WHO WILL BE ALIVE AT THE END OF TIME

It was reported from 'Abd Allāh ibn 'Amr that the Prophet (S) said, "The Hour will not come until Allah takes away the best people on earth; only the worst people will be left; they will not know any good or forbid any evil." (Aḥmad.)[1]

'Abd Allah ibn Mas'ūd said, "I heard the Prophet (S) say: 'Eloquence can be bewitching; the worst of the people are those upon whom the Hour will come while they are still alive, and those who turn graves into mosques'." (Aḥmad.)[2]

It was reported from Anas that the Prophet (S) said, "The Hour will not come until no-one on earth says '*Lā ilāha illā Allāh*'." (Aḥmad.)[3]

It was also reported from Anas that the Prophet (S) said: "The Hour will not come until no-one on earth says, 'Allah, Allah'." (Aḥmad.)[4]

There are two suggestions as to the meaning of the phrase, "until no-one on earth says 'Allah, Allah' ":

1. It could mean that no-one will forbid evil, or try to correct another if he sees him doing something wrong. We have already come across this in the *Ḥadīth* of 'Abd Allāh ibn 'Amr: "Only the worst people will be left; they will not know any good or forbid any evil".

2. It could mean that Allah will no longer be mentioned, and His Name will not be known; this will be part of the prevalent corruption and *Kufr*, as in the previous *Ḥadīth*, "Until no-one on earth says '*Lā ilāha illā Allah*' ".

'Ā'ishah said, "The Prophet (S) came in, saying 'O 'Ā'ishah, your people will be the first of my *Ummah* to join me.' When he sat down, I said, 'O Messenger of Allah, may I be sacrificed for you! When you came in, you were saying something which scared me'. He asked, 'What was that?' I said, 'You said that my people would be the first of your *Ummah* to join you'. He said, 'Yes'. I asked, 'Why is that?' He said, 'Death will be widespread among them, and their relatives will be jealous of them'. I said, 'How will people be after that?' He said, 'Like locusts: the strong will devour the weak, until the Hour comes' ". (Aḥmad.)[5]

'Albā' al-Salamī said, "I heard the Prophet (S) say: 'The Hour will only come upon the worst of the people' ". (Aḥmad.)[6]

**FOOTNOTES.**

1. Aḥmad, *Musnad*, 1/454.
2. *op. cit.,* 3/268.
3. *ibid.*
4. *op. cit.,* 3/107.
5. *op. cit.,* 6/81.
6. *op. cit.,* 3/499.